IMPACT LEADERSHIP

A STRATEGIC GUIDE TO SUSTAINABLE LEADERSHIP, ENHANCING TEAM ENGAGEMENT, AND LEADING WITH THE PRINCIPLE THAT PEOPLE ALWAYS MATTER

RON HARVEY

THREEFOLD
PUBLISHING

Copyright ©2025 by Ron Harvey

All rights reserved.

The content contained within this book may not be reproduced, duplicated or transmitted without direct written permission from the author or the publisher.

Under no circumstances will any blame or legal responsibility be held against the publisher, or author, for any damages, reparation, or monetary loss due to the information contained within this book. Either directly or indirectly. You are responsible for your own choices, actions, and results.

Legal Notice:

This book is copyright protected. This book is only for personal use. You cannot amend, distribute, sell, use, quote or paraphrase any part, or the content within this book, without the consent of the author or publisher.

Disclaimer Notice:

Please note the information contained within this document is for educational and entertainment purposes only. All effort has been executed to present accurate, up to date, and reliable, complete information. No warranties of any kind are declared or implied. Readers acknowledge that the author is not engaging in the rendering of legal, financial, medical or professional advice. The content within this book has been derived from various sources. Please consult a licensed professional before attempting any techniques outlined in this book.

By reading this document, the reader agrees that under no circumstances is the author responsible for any losses, direct or indirect, which are incurred as a result of the use of the information contained within this document, including, but not limited to, — errors, omissions, or inaccuracies.

CONTENTS

Foreword	v
Author's Note	ix
Introduction	xi

PART ONE
THE HEART OF LEADERSHIP

1. Trustworthy — The Foundation of Influence and Meaningful Relationships	3
2. Care — Leading with Compassion and Concern for People	11
3. Loving — Giving, Serving, and Uplifting Others	19
4. Encourager — Speaking Life into the Potential of Others	29

PART TWO
THE CHARACTER OF A LEADER

5. Accountability — Owning the Work and the Outcome	39
6. Humility — Staying Grounded While Reaching Higher	49
7. Servant Leadership — Putting People First to Build Lasting Impact	55
8. Listener — The Most Underrated Leadership Skill	65

PART THREE
THE COURAGE TO LEAD

9. Courage — Standing Strong in the Face of Adversity	75
10. Poised – Staying Grounded in Pressure	83
11. Passion – Leading with Fire, Energy, and Determination	93
12. Confident – Believing in Yourself So Others Can Too	101

PART FOUR
THE INFLUENCE OF PRESENCE

13. Approachable — Making Yourself Available to Your Team	111
14. Respect — Honoring People for Who They Are	119

15. Consistency — Showing Up with Steadiness and
    Intentionality ... 125
16. Presence — Be Where Your Feet Are ... 133

PART FIVE
THE LEGACY OF LEADERSHIP

17. Empowerment — Developing Leaders, Not Just
    Followers ... 141
18. Growth Mindset — Choosing Learning Over
    Limitation ... 149
19. Resilience — Leading Through Setbacks with
    Strength and Steadiness ... 155
20. Legacy — Leading Beyond Your Time ... 161

Conclusion: The Impact You Leave Behind ... 167
1. Citations ... 171

Author Biography ... 181

FOREWORD

While working as the Chief Operating Officer for the Charlotte Douglas International Airport, I was introduced to "Coach" Ron Harvey in my search for an executive coach. From the very beginning, I was struck by his authenticity, his calm yet confident demeanor, and the ease with which our conversations flowed. What began as a professional coaching relationship quickly became something more meaningful. Today, I am grateful to call Ron not only my executive coach, but also my mentor and friend. He has provided me with tremendous value in every one of those roles.

From those early conversations, it was clear that Ron's depth of leadership knowledge and experience extended far beyond anything I had encountered before. That depth—gained from years of active-duty military service and honed through time in both the public and private sectors—is not only impressive, but invaluable. I recognized immediately that his insights and perspectives were instruments I needed to add to my own leadership toolbox. What I have come to appreciate most, however, is not simply what Ron knows, but how he coaches: by asking the right questions, by listening intently, and by "holding up the mirror" so I could see myself more clearly—even when the reflection revealed my own blind spots.

Authentic leadership is reflective. Anyone who does not embrace that truth is missing the mark. Our teams, our legacy, and our ultimate value as leaders are not measured by the number of tasks we accomplish, but by how deeply we engage, connect, and develop the people entrusted to us. Leadership requires both courage and humility: the courage to act and the humility to look in the mirror and ask hard questions. Sometimes the reflection we see reveals the solution. Other times, it reveals the problem. The ability to face that reality, learn from it, and grow through it is what defines effective leaders.

Equally important is the recognition that every decision we make and every interaction we have leaves a mark. Leadership is never neutral. It always creates impact—positive or negative. Our leadership impact defines our legacy, and that legacy becomes the foundation on which others build. This is why Ron's work is so important, and why his philosophy—*People Always Matter*™—is more than a phrase. It is a compass.

With *Impact Leadership*, Ron distills years of experience into clear, practical, and transformational lessons. He doesn't just tell you how to lead—he shows you why your leadership matters, how it shapes lives, and how it can be sustained over time. From the Heart of Leadership to the Legacy of Leadership and everything in between, he invites you to unpack what it truly takes to lead not just today, but for years to come. And he has done so in a way that is both easy to consume and efficient to reference, ensuring that these lessons can travel with you throughout your leadership journey.

I have been fortunate to experience Ron's wisdom firsthand, and I can say with confidence that the principles in this book will challenge you, stretch you, and ultimately make you a better leader. They will remind you that leadership is not about the corner office or the title—it is about the lives you influence, the trust you build, and the legacy you leave behind.

I pray that you gain as much insight and value from this text as I have gained from Ron over the years. He has effectively summed up decades of leadership experience and presented it in a way that will equip you to reflect deeply, lead courageously, and build a legacy of lasting impact.

—Jerome D. Woodard
Chief Operating Officer – Charlotte Douglas International Airport

AUTHOR'S NOTE

I didn't set out to write just another leadership book.

I wrote *Impact Leadership* because, after decades of leading teams, coaching executives, and serving in both military and corporate environments, I've learned something that too many leaders forget:

People don't remember you for your title, your corner office, or the size of your budget.

They remember how you made them feel, how you showed up when it mattered most, and whether your leadership improved their lives or just added to their workload.

This book came from the thousands of conversations I've had with leaders at every level—from CEOs to frontline employees—when I asked one simple question: *Who has had the most significant impact on your life, and why?*

The answers were never about quarterly numbers or strategic plans. They were about trust, care, resilience, integrity, and encouragement, to name a few.

That's what impact leadership looks like. And that's what I want for you.

I want you to lead in a way that people will remember you for years to come—not because you were in charge, but because you made an impact. I want you to leave a legacy that is evident in the people you've developed, the culture you've created, and the lives you've influenced.

These pages aren't just theory—they're real-life experience. They come from my years in the U.S. Army, coaching leaders across different industries, and learning from my own mistakes, successes, and hard-earned lessons. You'll find stories, practical tools, and challenges made to help you lead with purpose and make a lasting impact.

So, as you read, I encourage you to do more than just underline or highlight. Apply these ideas in real situations. Use them in your meetings. Try them in difficult conversations. Practice them in your daily interactions.

Because the true measure of leadership isn't found in a book—it's found in the lives you touch and the impact you leave behind.

Lead well. Lead intentionally. And remember—People Always Matter.

— **Ron Harvey**

Author's Disclaimer

This is a work of nonfiction. While the core events, experiences, and insights are based on real people and circumstances, some names, identifying details, timelines, and locations have been changed to protect the privacy of individuals and organizations. In certain instances, stories have been adapted, compressed, or reconstructed from memory, interviews, and personal notes. Any composite characters or altered scenarios were created to preserve confidentiality or enhance narrative clarity, and they remain true in spirit to the actual events and lessons described. The intent is to honor the truth while respecting the dignity and discretion of those involved.

INTRODUCTION

What do we remember most about the people who changed our lives?

Over the past 15 years, I've asked thousands of people—including C-suite executives, frontline staff, educators, engineers, soldiers, nurses, and social workers—two deceptively simple questions:

1. Who is the one person who has had the most significant impact on who you are today?
2. What three words would you use to describe them?

Time and again, the answers people share reveal something deeply human. They don't mention accolades or technical skills. They don't recall degrees earned or awards received. Rarely do they mention a person's IQ, strategic insight, or professional titles.

Instead, they say:

Trustworthy. Honest. Compassionate. Supportive. Inspiring. Kind. Real.

These are not just buzzwords—they are proven game changers.

They don't appear on résumés or LinkedIn endorsements, but they are written on people's hearts. They are the quiet qualities that resonate in a world often distracted by noise.

And they are the fingerprints of impact—the evidence left behind by someone who didn't just lead but truly cared.

In every setting where I've asked these questions—whether over coffee in a breakroom, on stage in front of thousands, or during quiet one-on-one coaching conversations—the same pattern appears. When people think about who truly influenced them, they don't remember what the person did as much as how that person made them feel. This isn't anecdotal—it's strongly supported by neuroscience.

Research in cognitive psychology and neurobiology shows that the brain's emotional centers, especially the amygdala and hippocampus, are crucial for memory formation. Experiences filled with emotion—particularly positive feelings like empathy, respect, or kindness—are remembered more deeply and recalled more vividly. In essence, emotional resonance leaves lasting impressions. As Maya Angelou wisely said, "People will forget what you said, people will forget what you did, but people will never forget how you made them feel."

This insight has allowed me to positively impact others as a leader for decades.

In a world obsessed with performance, productivity, and prestige, it turns out that what people truly value in their leaders, mentors, and influencers has nothing to do with status—and everything to do with presence.

That's when it hit me: leadership isn't defined by your title, your résumé, or your social media profile. It's defined by your impact.

And your impact is shaped—every day—by your behavior.

Not the carefully scripted behavior shown in keynote speeches or quarterly reports, but the consistent, daily choices you make in how you treat people, listen, show up, and lead under pressure.

That's where true leadership happens. In the hallways. In the emails. In the in-between.

This book was inspired by those words—those soul-words that hundreds of people have shared during moments of quiet reflection and heartfelt honesty. Collected over years of inquiry, these words lay the framework for what I call Impact Leadership.

Each chapter focuses on one of these key traits—not as an abstract idea, but as a lived value. These qualities inspire trust, foster belonging, and leave a legacy of influence that extends far beyond the boardroom or office.

Impact Leadership isn't about impressing others.

It's leadership that endures. It's leadership that transforms.

It's leadership that changes lives—starting with yours.

Why does this matter now? Because we are living in a time when leadership is being redefined right before our eyes. The old paradigms—focused on command-and-control, charisma over character, and optics over authenticity—are breaking down. We crave something deeper, more genuine.

Across every sector and industry, a significant shift is happening. The Edelman Trust Barometer consistently shows that trust in institutions and traditional authority figures is decreasing. At the same time, expectations for leaders are increasing; people want leaders who are transparent, accountable, and genuine. According to Gallup, nearly 70% of employee engagement depends on the manager's behavior. Engagement, retention, innovation — it all comes from the relationships a leader builds.

In high-trust workplaces, as explained in Harvard Business Review, employees report:

- 74% less stress
- 106% more energy at work
- 50% higher productivity
- 13% fewer sick days

Trust isn't a soft metric—it's a key driver of performance. It is earned not through speeches or slogans, but through consistency, humility, vulnerability, and humanity.

So if you're a senior executive trying to build a culture that attracts and motivates talent…

If you're a new manager navigating the challenges of leading your peers…

If you're a teacher shaping the hearts and minds of the next generation…

If you're a coach, a parent, a pastor, or a public servant—this book is for you.

It's an invitation:

- To lead more intentionally.
- To live more authentically.
- To serve more humanely.
- And to remember that every interaction is a chance to either build or break trust.

You don't have to be perfect.
You don't need all the answers.
You just need to care enough to show up.
Care enough to be present when it would be easier to retreat.
Care enough to listen when it would be quicker to talk.
Care enough to lead with purpose instead of ego.

Because the truth is, we are always leading—through our actions, tone, and choices. The question isn't whether you're making an impact, but what kind of impact you're making. So, let's start this journey together.

One word at a time.
One quality at a time.
One moment of presence, compassion, and courage at a time.
The legacy of your leadership is not built in a day.
But it is built each day.

PART ONE
THE HEART OF LEADERSHIP

CHAPTER 1
TRUSTWORTHY – THE FOUNDATION OF INFLUENCE AND MEANINGFUL RELATIONSHIPS

I'VE COME to believe that trust is the difference between being in charge and being followed.

It doesn't matter how compelling your strategy is or how much authority your title has—if people don't trust you, they'll nod politely and then quietly disengage. I've seen it in boardrooms and breakrooms. I've seen it in client relationships, internal teams, and executive partnerships. Trust is the invisible thread that decides whether people simply follow orders or are fully committed. Trust lets people give their best consistently, and it helps you tackle the toughest tasks when things get complicated.

LEADERSHIP SNAPSHOT

When Alan Mulally became Ford's CEO, he started each meeting by inviting leaders to share their thoughts and ideas. This method promoted collaboration and built a trusted environment where everyone felt valued and heard. It encouraged sharing real problems, not just good news. This move toward transparency and accountability helped rebuild trust across the company and ultimately saved Ford during the financial crisis.

OPENING THOUGHT

People don't follow those they don't trust. Period.

You can be brilliant, charismatic, and strategic, but none of that matters if your team doesn't trust you.

WHY THIS MATTERS

Early in my career as a soldier, I learned that you can't force influence. You either earn it through trust, or you spend your energy trying to make up for its lack. There's a clear difference between a team that feels compelled to act and one that wants to do so—because they trust you, believe in you, and understand the mission. Trust enables others to be vulnerable and stay engaged for longer periods.

High-trust environments aren't just more pleasant workplaces—they perform better. Period. The evidence is clear. Studies by Gallup (2023) and Kouzes & Posner (2017) show that high-trust organizations have notably higher retention rates, greater engagement scores, and outperform low-trust cultures in productivity metrics across the board.

When trust exists, communication flows more easily. Turnover decreases. Decision-making becomes quicker. People take ownership because they feel seen, heard, respected, and safe. They are willing to bring their whole selves to the table.

But without it? The easy things become complicated, and the complex stuff gets avoided if possible.

WHAT THIS IS (AND ISN'T)

Let me make this clear: trust isn't about charisma. It's not about having the right personality, being everyone's friend, or delivering inspiring speeches. Trust is built one moment at a time—through consistent, honest, transparent, and reliable actions.

Trust isn't blind loyalty. It's not about people never questioning you. In fact, high-trust cultures often have more disagreement because people feel safe enough to share their views. Trust isn't a get-out-of-jail-free card for bad decisions or poor leadership. It's earned—and delicate.

It's the currency we all use, whether we realize it or not. Every collaboration, partnership, sale, and conversation quietly ask: *Can I trust you? Will you do what you say? Are you who you claim to be?*

WHAT IT LOOKS LIKE

Let me describe a scenario. When trust exists in leadership, it appears as follows:

- Video matches your Audio—even when it's inconvenient.
- You show up on time every time, prepared and present.
- When plans change, you should communicate that early, clearly, frequently, and honestly.
- You don't play favorites. Your team sees fairness in your decisions.
- When you mess up, you own up to it, and you clean it up.
- You give credit when things go right—and accept responsibility when they don't.
- What you say reflects how you live publicly and privately.

People don't just listen to what you say. They observe what you do. That consistency is where trust resides.

I once worked with a mid-sized company where the CEO proudly stated that transparency was a core value. However, major decisions were made behind closed doors, information was kept at the top, and junior staff members were often caught off guard. No one said it openly, but the culture shouted: "Don't believe what's on the wall—believe what you see."

That's the thing about trust. It can't be claimed. It must be proven.

WHAT HAPPENS WITHOUT IT

When trust breaks down, the results are quick and damaging. People may not leave immediately—but they begin to pull back emotionally.

You'll notice it first in meetings: fewer ideas and more guarded answers. Silence replaces creativity. People wait to see what "the boss" wants instead of sharing their best thinking.

Then the team chemistry shifts. People become transactional. They'll tolerate you—but not follow you. Turnover increases. Dysfunction begins to occur.

And this is what hurts the most: the people who stay begin working around you, not with you. They avoid conversations. They stop bringing issues to you. You're still in charge, but you've lost your influence.

That was my experience in one of my first leadership roles.

CASE-IN-POINT: LEARNING IT THE HARD WAY

I was in my late twenties when I was asked to lead a small but talented team as a newly promoted leader. I had the credentials, the confidence, and the work ethic. I felt like I was ready.

I believed I had trust because of my position/title, and the people who put me there believed in me.

My team wasn't performing well, and I couldn't understand why they seemed so disengaged. They completed the work, but the energy was low, and they only did the bare minimum. There was no sense of ownership or extra effort. The culture felt purely transactional. They weren't fully committed.

So, I did what many new leaders do: I tried to push harder. More meetings. Tighter deadlines. More motivational speeches. I tried to bargain with them and persuade them to follow me.

None of it worked.

Eventually, I pulled one of my mentors aside and asked, "What am I missing?"

He looked at me for a moment and said, "You aren't listening to your people, and they don't trust you yet. You talk a lot, but you don't follow through. And when things get hard, you are avoiding them and not addressing them in a timely manner."

That was a punch to the gut, and my ego took a hit. But he was right.

I hadn't fully been where my feet were. I was leading from a distance—promising support I wasn't actually giving, arriving late to team huddles like I had all the answers, and vanishing when I felt uncomfortable. I wasn't consistent. I wasn't truly present. I wasn't dependable. I hadn't earned their trust.

It wasn't my skills or experience that were in question—it was my character.

From that moment, I changed how I led. I started listening more. I stopped making promises unless I was 100% sure I could keep them. I showed up early, stayed late when needed, and admitted when I didn't know something. I didn't expect trust to return overnight—but over time, it did.

The culture shifted. People leaned in again. Ideas resurfaced. My team didn't just execute the work—they began to own it, and they gave me the chance to lead.

All because of trust.

HOW TO BUILD IT

So, how do you build trust—especially if it's been broken?

Here's what I've learned, both personally and professionally, from serving and coaching dozens of executives:

1. Own your mistakes first.
Don't wait to be called out. When you blow it, acknowledge it

quickly, clearly, and without excuse. "That was my fault" is a powerful trust-building phrase.

2. Be where you said you'd be.
If you say you'll be at the team check-in, be there. Show up consistently. Presence signals priority.

3. Say "I don't know" when you genuinely don't have an answer.
Pretending to know everything damages your credibility. Being honest about uncertainty is respectful—and people appreciate it.

4. Handle conflict respectfully and promptly.
Avoiding tension doesn't maintain peace—it simply postpones a bigger breakdown. Tackle issues head-on, but with respect. People trust leaders who confront tough issues.

5. Share the "why," not just the "what."
Don't just dictate—invite others to provide feedback early and often. When people understand the reasons behind decisions, they feel involved and respected, even if they don't completely agree.

6. Always come through.
Do what you say you'll do, no matter how small. Each time you follow through, you earn more trust. Conversely, when you drop the ball without acknowledgment, you create doubt and weaken the trust you've worked so hard to build.

Trust isn't built through grand gestures. It's built through small moments—again, and again, and again.

This is what transforms managers into leaders, teams into families, clients into lifelong advocates, and influence into something that lasts a lifetime.

So, if you want to be trusted, be trustworthy. Start here: Be consistent, be present, be honest, and be vulnerable.

And above all, be someone others can rely on. Always.

TEAM APPLICATION

- Ask: "What does trust from me look like to you?"
- Serve others and not yourself.
- Model vulnerability at your next team meeting.

LEADER'S JOURNAL

Recall a time when a leader broke your trust. How did it affect your engagement?

TEAM CHALLENGE

In your next meeting, ask each team member to share one behavior that builds trust for them.

LEADERSHIP REFLECTION

What's one thing you have done recently that built or broke trust?

ONE-LINER TO REMEMBER

"You don't get to decide if you're trusted—your actions do."

CHAPTER 2
CARE — LEADING WITH COMPASSION AND CONCERN FOR PEOPLE

I USED to believe that performance and achieving results were all that mattered. I was trained to think that way, coached to meet targets, and rewarded for outcomes. But as I grew and led others — delving deeper into leadership, culture, and people — I realized something powerful: Performance isn't just about metrics; it's about connection, and connection is rooted in caring about people.

I don't mean a surface-level, check-the-box kind of care. I mean the kind that sees people, knows people, supports people, and honors their whole humanity—not just their job title and what they can do for you. That kind of care builds bonds. And those bonds are what hold teams together under pressure and push them higher during the wins. That kind of care gives you more than what the job description requires or could ever ask for.

LEADERSHIP SNAPSHOT:

Indra Nooyi, former CEO of PepsiCo, wrote personal letters to the parents of her senior executives, thanking them for raising such talented leaders. This act of care built deep loyalty and engagement throughout the company.

OPENING THOUGHT

If people don't feel like you care about them, they will eventually stop caring about the work.

WHY THIS MATTERS

The top-performing teams I've seen all share one thing in common: they felt safe, heard, respected, and appreciated. Not just managed—but genuinely cared for. And science confirms this. According to a Gallup workplace study, employees who strongly agree that their leader, supervisor, or someone at work cares about them as a person are 69% less likely to actively seek a new job. Let that sink in. It's not a bonus, a free lunch, or a great breakroom. It's feeling cared for and appreciated that drives results and keeps people around.

And it's not just about staying—it's about showing up. A 2021 study published in the Harvard Business Review found that when employees perceive high levels of compassion from leadership, they are more engaged, collaborative, and committed to the organization's success. In my experience, care unlocks discretionary effort—the willingness to go above and beyond not because you have to, but because you want to. That's the magic zone. That's where trust meets motivation, and teams thrive.

WHAT THIS IS (AND ISN'T)

Let me clarify something: care is not coddling or hand holding. It's not about lowering standards. In fact, it's the opposite. Care means noticing and responding to people's needs respectfully so they can rise to meet the challenge. It's asking, "What support do you need to be successful?" instead of saying, "Figure it out."

Care is a strategy. A *human* strategy.

It's not weakness—it's leadership. The kind of leadership that intentionally creates space for others to be brilliant and innovative. I once coached a senior executive who told me, "I don't want to get too close to my team. I might lose my edge." What he didn't realize was that his distance was costing him the ability to have a more meaningful impact on others. People didn't trust him. They complied but didn't commit. When he finally started showing up with curiosity and concern— not just commands— everything changed. I learned that to secure a job or position, I needed to demonstrate my expertise and produce the required credentials to prove it. However, to lead people effectively, I had to care for them and their success genuinely.

Caring isn't about being soft. It's about being smart and staying connected.

WHAT IT LOOKS LIKE

Here's what caring in action looks like. I've seen it firsthand, through the people who shaped me. My grandfather, John Robert Evans Sr., started a church in 1925 that still stands today—a place where people found hope, belonging, and faith through every season. My grandmother opened one of the first private kindergartens in our community, giving Black children the chance to learn to read when no one else would. And my parents, with only 18 years of formal education between them, raised twelve children and managed to build a thriving business, serve others, and become key figures in our community.

They taught me that care is not just a feeling; it's a decision you make every day to show up for people, lift them when they're weary, and create opportunities where none exist. Their legacy reminds us that true leadership begins with the courage to care and help others.

You know your people's names, strengths, and goals. It may sound simple, but I've seen too many leaders refer to employees as headcounts or roles. The best leaders take the time to understand what motivates each person. They know who's taking night classes, who's working to buy their first home, and who wants to transition into a new department. They gather this information because they genuinely care enough to ask.

You notice when something's off—and you check in. One of the most respected leaders I ever worked with had a habit of walking through the motor pool not to monitor, but to connect. He'd stop by desks, not with tasks, but with questions like, "You seem quieter than usual—how are you holding up?" That kind of presence is irreplaceable. It tells people they matter beyond their to-do list or day-to-day job.

You protect well-being, not just output. That means being aware of signs of burnout, speaking up when workloads are excessive, and advocating for healthy boundaries. When care is shown, people feel like their well-being is just as important as their performance.

You listen deeply and respond personally. I'm talking about genuine listening—the kind that doesn't start formulating a response while the other person is still speaking. When a team member approaches you with an issue, they're not just seeking a solution; they're seeking to be heard. A study from the Center for Creative Leadership found that leaders who genuinely listen are rated as much more effective than those who don't. Listening is authentic care at its core.

WHAT HAPPENS WITHOUT IT

When care is missing, people don't always leave—they become disengaged. They show up but not fully committed. They stop sharing ideas and taking risks. They quietly quit. The term "quiet quitting" gained popularity after the pandemic, but I've observed it for years—people doing only the bare minimum, not out of laziness, but because no one made them feel it was worth going the extra mile.

Even if productivity stays high for a while, morale declines.

Burnout spreads. People start feeling like mere cogs in a machine. I once advised a fast-growing tech startup where the CEO boasted about how hard everyone worked—50-hour weeks were typical. "We're dominating the market," he told me. But when I spoke with his staff, the word I heard most often wasn't "driven." It was "exhausted." A year later, half of his leadership team had quit.

When care is absent, people feel replaceable. And when they believe they are replaceable, they stop giving their best. Most businesses cannot afford that kind of loss.

HOW TO BUILD IT

You don't build a culture of care with a memo. You build it with moments—small, consistent moments that add up over time. Here's how:

1. Be Present

Presence is the foundation of good care. When you're in a meeting, stay engaged. When someone is talking to you, put down your phone. Presence shows value. It says, "This matters to me. You matter to me." A University of Michigan study on leader presence found that perceived attentiveness was directly linked to trust in teams. Presence isn't just a perk—it's power.

2. Lead with Heart, Not Just Policy

Policy is important, but it's not enough. People want to understand why decisions are made and that their humanity is recognized. I once worked with a leader who followed every policy flawlessly but left people feeling cold. Why? Because she never paused to explain, empathize, or connect. Heart doesn't mean abandoning rules—it means applying them with empathy.

3. Schedule Check-ins That Aren't About Tasks

This is one of the simplest changes that has the biggest impact. Regular check-ins—just to ask how someone is really doing—are powerful. They don't have to be long. Ten minutes of sincere conversation can do more to boost engagement than any performance dashboard. I've tried this in dozens of organizations, and the results are always the same: morale improves, and turnover decreases.

4. Support Through Challenges

Caring doesn't mean fixing everything — it means standing beside people as they navigate it. That could mean flexibility during a family crisis, grace in the face of a mistake, or encouragement during a tough assignment. One leader I admire says, "I'll never lower the bar, but I'll always lengthen the ladder." That's care. High expectations with strong support.

5. Give Praise That's Personal

Generic praise doesn't resonate. "Good job" is acceptable, but it doesn't motivate people. What does? Praise that's specific, personal, and aligned with values. Instead of "Great work," try "The way you handled that client—staying calm, listening, and finding a creative solution—was a perfect example of the empathy we say we value here." That kind of recognition nurtures people.

6. Remember the Details

Birthdays, work anniversaries, the name of someone's dog—these things matter more than you realize. When you notice small details, you send a powerful message: "You're not just a role. You're a person I care about." One executive I coached made it a point to write handwritten cards for every employee's birthday— more than 100 in total. When I asked why, she said, "I want them to remember that I saw them and know that I value them."

And they did.

THE ROI OF CARE

I've seen companies turn around completely—not because of new strategy decks, but because of new energy. That energy comes from leaders choosing to show up differently and to care.

One healthcare organization I worked with experienced chronic turnover among its nursing staff. After a leadership retreat that focused on empathy, personal connection, and team recognition, turnover decreased by 35% within a year. Patient satisfaction improved because the staff felt valued by leadership once again. Why? Because people who feel cared for tend to care for others better—and this positive cycle spreads.

In another case, a public service firm began weekly "coffee and care" chats—voluntary, non-agenda check-ins with leadership. Within six months, employee engagement scores rose from 58% to 82%. Nothing else changed—just how people felt.

FINAL THOUGHTS

I'll leave you with this: People will leave their jobs if their leaders don't care about them. If you want performance, you need people. And if you want people to stay, grow, and give their best — you need care. Not just in your words, but in your actions. Not just in policies, but in practice. In today's world, care isn't a soft skill. It's a survival skill. It's how you build culture, trust, and legacy. It's how you lead consistently. So ask yourself: Who have I seen today? Who have I checked in with — not for status, but for wellness? Who have I encouraged, acknowledged, and supported? Because leadership isn't a title; it's a relationship. And relationships thrive when we care about people.

TEAM APPLICATION

- Ask: "What support do you need from me right now?"
- Celebrate unseen effort.

- Protect personal check-in time during meetings.
- Practice compassion in decision-making, especially under pressure.

LEADER'S JOURNAL

Who might be feeling overlooked on your team, and how will you address it?

TEAM CHALLENGE

Ask every team member to share one way they feel most supported at work.

LEADERSHIP REFLECTION

Who might be feeling unseen on your team, and what will you do about it?

ONE-LINER TO REMEMBER

When people see that you care, they tend to care more about the work, the team, and the mission.

CHAPTER 3
LOVING — GIVING, SERVING, AND UPLIFTING OTHERS

I WAS TOLD that love doesn't belong in business.

As a young leader, I was taught to value logic, strategy, and efficiency. I believed my role was to get things done at all costs, develop KPIs, and help the organization grow. Talking about love That was for therapists and poets, not battlefields or boardrooms.

But years in the trenches and great mentors shaped me.

I've guided leaders through layoffs, expansions, burnout crises, and cultural collapses. I've seen companies with cutting-edge tech fail because their people didn't feel cared for—and I've seen struggling nonprofits thrive because their leaders led with heart. I've come to understand and believe this: Love ranks among the top five most underused traits in leadership.

OPENING THOUGHT

Impact leadership is grounded in love. It involves showing up for others with dedication, compassion, and care.

WHY THIS MATTERS

Love transforms organizations from mechanical to meaningful, turning workplace transactions into human connections. Moreover, it's effective.

According to a Harvard Business Review study by Sigal Barsade and Olivia A. O'Neill (2014), workplaces characterized by companionate love—defined as affection, compassion, and caring—show higher employee satisfaction, better teamwork, and lower absenteeism rates. The findings weren't limited to nonprofits or mission-driven sectors; even high-pressure industries like healthcare and finance experienced positive outcomes.

Jim Collins, in Good to Great, wrote that leaders of lasting organizations are characterized by what he calls "Level 5 Leadership"—a paradoxical blend of humility and strong determination. Humility, he discovered, often appears in very human, compassionate leadership that puts people before ego.

In my career, spanning over 35 years, I have seen time and again that leaders who genuinely care for their people build teams that are sustainable and consistently exceed expectations.

WHAT IT LOOKS LIKE

1. People go the extra mile—not for attention, but for the leader and the mission.

A 2020 Deloitte study found that 79% of employees who felt their leaders cared about their well-being reported higher engagement and were more likely to stay long-term. Love in leadership isn't about feel-good slogans—it's about action.

When I assumed responsibility over my first company as a First Sergeant, I was eager but also nervous. I understood the responsibility wasn't just about formations, inspections, or completing missions. It was about people. It was about setting the standard, being the shield, and acting as the advocate when needed.

Soon after I arrived, a Soldier caught my attention who was in serious trouble. He had made a mistake—one that could have ended his career. The previous leader was ready to abandon him, seeing him as a liability rather than as a human being who had made a mistake.

Before making any decisions, I did what I believe leaders are supposed to do: I listened. I sat down with the Soldier, looked him in the eyes, and told him I wasn't there to judge him but to understand him. I asked him to tell me what happened, and more importantly, why it happened. I spoke with his peers, his squad leader, and even those outside his immediate circle. I observed how he carried himself and how he treated others when he thought no one was watching.

After my own investigation, I concluded that this Soldier didn't need to be discarded. He needed leadership. But more than that, he needed to know we loved and valued him.

Not the soft, emotional love many misunderstand, but *love in action*: accountability, belief in his worth, and a commitment to his growth even when it was uncomfortable. Love meant not giving him the easy way out but standing by him as he took responsibility and rebuilt his reputation. Love meant seeing who he *could* become, not just who he was in that moment of failure.

So, we made a plan together: clear expectations, honest conversations, daily check-ins, and extra responsibilities that let him contribute while earning back trust. I told him, "Your career isn't over. You've been given a chance, and you will need to work harder than ever to prove you're worth the trust we're placing in you."

And he did. This Soldier responded in a way that reminded me why I wanted to lead in the first place. He showed up early, volunteered for tough details, led from the front, and helped others who were struggling—remembering how it felt when he was the one almost written off.

Over time, he became one of the best Soldiers in the unit, respected by his peers and trusted by his leaders. Watching him transform wasn't just a win for him; it was a win for the entire formation and his family. It reinforced to me that leadership isn't about punishing people for failing; it's about helping them get back up so they can learn to stand taller.

That is what love looks like in leadership. It's patient, but it is also honest. It encourages people to grow while walking alongside them. It holds people accountable while reminding them they are not alone. It sees the person inside the uniform and says, "You matter, and I won't give up on you."

Just like a plant manager I once coached, who chose to walk the floor with his team during the toughest weeks instead of hiding in meetings, I learned that leaders don't disappear when people need them most. They show up, observe, listen, care, and lead.

Because love is not a sign of weakness in leadership. It is the quiet strength that says, "I will stand with you while you get this right," and it is what turns mistakes into momentum, struggles into stories of redemption, and teams into families.

That is the power of love in leadership.

My secret? "I just try to treat them the way I'd want someone to treat my kids at their jobs."

That's love—in—action.

2. You extend grace when others fall short.

We all make mistakes. The question is: how do we respond?

Psychologist Carol Dweck's research on growth mindset shows that environments where failure is accepted without fear are more likely to foster creativity and learning (Dweck, 2006). When leaders respond with empathy rather than punishment, they create a climate where risk-taking and innovation can flourish.

I remember a CFO I worked with who noticed that a young

accountant analyst had accidentally sent out incorrect financial data. Instead of reprimanding him, she called him in and reviewed the numbers with him, step by step. Later, she shared with me, "That was an investment in his future. He'll never forget this mistake—or that I had his back."

And he didn't. He was promoted within the year—and stayed at the company another seven years.

3. You show up in life's most challenging moments.

This is where love reveals itself.

I once worked with a nonprofit that served youth. The executive director, Julia, led with extraordinary heart. When a team member lost her mother, Julia didn't just send flowers. She stepped in to assist with that person's grant reports, organized meal deliveries, and offered her paid time off, even though the organization was small and underfunded.

It wasn't just kindness; it was love shown through logistics and practical support.

Her actions didn't go unnoticed by the team. Their annual employee engagement survey—conducted through Gallup—ranked in the 90th percentile for "I feel someone at work cares about me." Unsurprisingly, they also had the highest retention rate among similar nonprofits in the region.

4. You elevate others without needing the credit.

True love in leadership is *secure*. It doesn't hoard spotlight or demand applause.

One of my favorite examples is Cheryl Bachelder, former CEO of Popeyes Louisiana Kitchen. When she took over, the brand was struggling. Her philosophy? "Serve the people who serve the guests." She emphasized servant leadership—not just as a catchphrase, but as a way of life.

By shifting the focus from control to care, she saw same-store sales increase for eight straight years, and the stock quadrupled in value. In her book Dare to Serve, she describes how putting love at the heart of leadership created not only a thriving culture but also a booming business.

WHAT HAPPENS WITHOUT IT

Organizations that lack love aren't always broken. Sometimes, they're simply cold and transactional.

1. Cold, transactional relationships.

Transactional leadership—focused on rules, contracts, and performance-based rewards—can lead to short-term improvements. However, over time, it alienates employees. A 2021 McKinsey study found that the top reason people leave their jobs isn't pay—it's not feeling valued.

Where love is absent, people stop bringing their whole selves to work. They do what's required and nothing more.

2. Trust fractures.

Without love, trust decays.

Organizational psychologist Amy Edmondson introduced the term psychological safety to describe environments where people feel comfortable speaking up. Her research at Google revealed that the highest-performing teams weren't those with the most talent—but those built on the most trust.

Trust is built when people feel loved—seen, safe, heard, and supported. When that's lacking, people hoard information, withhold feedback, are not creative or innovative, and brace for blame.

3. Burnout rises.

A Gallup study in 2023 confirmed that a lack of emotional support from leaders is one of the top five reasons for employee burnout. When people feel used instead of valued, they lose energy and begin to disengage.

4. Innovation diminishes.

Innovation demands risk. Risk calls for safety. And safety, as every child learns before every adult forgets, stems from love.

In one Fortune 100 company I serve, the engineering team faced a creative block. Fear of criticism was widespread. After a leadership shift focused on empathy, recognition, and collaborative support, the number of patents submitted increased the following year. That wasn't a change in talent — it was a change in emotional climate.

CASE-IN-POINT: WHEN LOVE BECOMES CULTURE

I return often to the story of Julia, the nonprofit director.

She didn't just lead with love—she cultivated a culture rooted in love. It became part of decision-making, policies, and even onboarding.

When new hires started, they weren't just given manuals—they were paired with mentors who checked in weekly. Annual reviews included not only performance goals but also well-being questions: "What brings you joy in your work?" "What support do you need next quarter?"

Her philosophy: "No one should have to leave their humanity at the door to do good work."

That mindset not only felt good—it also delivered results. Their clients' outcomes improved, their funding increased, and their staff became the organization's most effective recruiters.

Love, it turned out, wasn't fluff. It was a competitive edge.

HOW TO BUILD IT

Building a loving culture requires intentional effort. Here's how I support my clients in getting started:

1. Prioritize people first—even if it inconveniences you.
Resist the urge to dehumanize just to move faster. Always talk to people before making decisions about them. When unsure, take a moment to ask: "What's the impact on the people we serve and lead?"

2. Be there when life gets messy.
You don't need perfect words. You just need to show up. A leader who appears during grief, illness, anxiety, or chaos earns trust that lasts beyond any fiscal year.

3. Prioritize creating space for humanity, not merely for productivity.
Schedule breaks. Normalize rest. Celebrate real-life moments—birthdays, family milestones, even tough anniversaries. Show people they're more than what they produce.

4. Choose to find the best in others.
Default to trusting others' good intentions. When something goes wrong, ask first: "Are you okay?" before "What happened?"
This doesn't mean avoiding accountability. It means leading with compassion *before* correction.

5. Ensure people understand they matter.
Recognition shouldn't be rare. Neuroscientific research by Teresa Amabile shows that recognizing progress is one of the most powerful motivators at work (Harvard Business Review, 2011). A quick thank-you email. A spontaneous shout-out in a team meeting. A hand-written note. These moments, when genuine, are acts of love.

FINAL THOUGHT

Love isn't weak. It isn't soft. It's not something to force into your culture after the real work is finished.

Love *is* the work.

It's what fosters belonging. It's what maintains trust. It's what gives people the courage to innovate, the strength to endure, and the will to care for each other in return.

In my early days of consulting, I helped organizations operate more effectively. Now, I help them love better—and they still operate more effectively.

So, ask yourself, as a leader, a colleague, and a builder of teams:

What would it look like to lead with love today?

Who needs your patience, your presence, or your uplifting word?

How might your culture change if people knew—*really knew*—that they mattered?

Because when we lead with love, we don't just change organizations.

We change lives.

TEAM APPLICATION

- Ask: "What's one thing I do that helps you feel supported?"
- Call out acts of care and service publicly.
- Connect team goals to the greater mission.

LEADERSHIP REFLECTION

How am I ensuring my leadership demonstrates love in action?

ONE-LINER TO REMEMBER

"Love isn't soft leadership—it's the strongest form of service."

CHAPTER 4
ENCOURAGER — SPEAKING LIFE INTO THE POTENTIAL OF OTHERS

I'VE SAT in boardrooms with Fortune 500 executives and walked floors with line workers wearing steel-toed boots and name tags. I've coached entrepreneurs striving for their first big break and leaders trying to hold onto the ground they've already gained. Throughout it all, one truth has become clear: every person you lead is fighting a battle you can't see.

They might not show it. They may wear a mask of competence or confidence. But underneath? There are doubts, fears, insecurities—questions about whether they're good enough, capable enough, or simply enough.

That's why encouragement matters more than we often realize.

Encouragement doesn't remove the obstacles people face, but it does give them the strength to keep going. It doesn't fix every problem, but it gives them the courage to confront it directly. It turns trembling legs into confident strides.

As a leadership consultant, I used to believe my main role was strategy—analyzing metrics, streamlining operations, and planning paths for growth. But over time, I've realized that to transform an organization, you need to start by changing how people see themselves within it. When leaders inspire their teams, they unlock something that strategy alone can't: belief.

And belief? That transforms everything.

LEADERSHIP SNAPSHOT:

When Howard Schultz returned as CEO of Starbucks, he made a point to personally thank and encourage frontline baristas and store managers-often with handwritten notes. This culture of encouragement helped Starbucks rebound from crisis, reigniting morale and performance across thousands of locations.

OPENING THOUGHT

Encouragement is like oxygen for the soul.

It reminds people of who they are and who they're becoming.

THE DATA BEHIND ENCOURAGEMENT

Let's ground this in something concrete. According to Gallup's 2023 State of the Workplace Report, employees who get regular recognition and encouragement are four times more likely to be engaged at work and 44% more likely to stay with their company. Engagement isn't just a luxury—it's essential for performance, innovation, and loyalty.

This doesn't mean throwing around shallow praise like confetti. Real encouragement is specific, timely, and rooted in honesty. It's not flattery. It's not ego-stroking. It's not a manipulative tactic to "get more" from people.

It's leadership.

True encouragement means telling someone: 'I see what's in you—even if you don't yet."

WHAT ENCOURAGEMENT *IS* (AND *ISN'T*)

Encouragement involves recognizing and naming growth, effort, and character—not just outcomes. It highlights qualities that might otherwise be overlooked: perseverance despite failure, compassion during conflicts, and quiet excellence in a noisy world.

Encouragement is not:

- Generic praise like "Good job!" without context.
- A once-a-year performance review pat on the back.
- A sandwich technique where you soften hard feedback with a fake compliment upfront.

It is:

- Authentic.
- Tailored to the person and the moment.
- Delivered with intention, not obligation.

WHAT IT LOOKS LIKE IN PRACTICE

A few years back, I worked with a mid-size tech company experiencing rapid growth. The CEO was brilliant but admittedly found it challenging to lead people. I watched him during a team meeting, where a junior developer nervously presented a prototype. It wasn't perfect—but it showed initiative.

After the meeting, I pulled the CEO aside and asked, "What did you think?"

He said, "I mean, it wasn't bad. But it had issues."

I asked, "Did you see how nervous he was?"

He nodded.

"And did you notice he stayed late last week trying to prep for this?"

The CEO blinked. "I didn't know that."

"You don't have to ignore the flaws," I said, "but imagine what happens if you start with encouragement: 'I saw how much effort you put into this. That initiative matters.'"

He tried it.

The next day, he sent the developer a short email:

"I noticed the time and care you put into your presentation. It shows you're growing fast. Let's keep building on that."

Three months later, that same developer was leading a team of interns and delivering features faster than ever. Not because of the email—but because of the belief it inspired.

Encouragement doesn't manufacture talent. But it draws it out.

WHAT HAPPENS WITHOUT IT

Organizations that withhold encouragement aren't always toxic, but they often feel uninspired and quietly disengaged. They function, but do not flourish.

Here's what I've seen, again and again:

- Talented people feel unseen.
- They stop offering ideas. They play it safe.
- Burnout builds silently.
- Without acknowledgment, effort starts to feel invisible. Exhaustion creeps in.
- Confidence erodes.
- Without encouragement, self-doubt becomes the loudest voice in the room.
- Teams perform well… but never stretch.

Fear of failure often overcomes the desire to innovate.

Reflect on your own life. Can you recall a moment when someone said something simple—but timely—that kept you going?

That's the power you hold, as a leader, in every conversation.

HOW TO LEAD AS AN ENCOURAGER

So, how do we go about doing it?

1. Speak specifically.
Don't just say, "Great job." Say, "I noticed how you stayed calm during that heated client call. That's leadership."

2. Acknowledge the small wins others miss.
Big wins get media attention. But small wins create momentum. Highlight them.

3. Write short notes or voice memos.
A sticky note on a desk. A 30-second voicemail. A quick Slack message. Encouragement doesn't need a stage.

4. Affirm people publicly, coach privately.
Celebrate effort publicly, but give constructive feedback privately.

5. Believe in people, especially on the hard days.
Anyone can cheer during a victory lap. The best leaders step up when the scoreboard is against you.
Encouragement isn't a one-time gesture—it's a rhythm.

CASE-IN-POINT: THE HANDWRITTEN NOTE

One of the most influential leaders I ever coached always made it a point to leave handwritten notes for his team. He told me, "People remember paper."

One day, a new hire—fresh out of college—found a note on his desk after a challenging first week. It read:

Your eye for detail improved our work today. That made a difference. Thank you.

Years passed. That employee rose through the ranks, led new

teams, and won awards. Years later, at a conference, he pulled that note from his wallet—creased and worn, but intact.

"This reminded me I belonged," he said. "Before I even believed it myself."

That's the kind of leader I want to be. The kind whose words stay in someone's wallet—not because they were poetic, but because they were *true*.

WHY THIS MATTERS (MORE THAN EVER)

In a world of automation, remote work, and digital communication, the human element has never been more vital. Algorithms don't motivate. AI doesn't understand heart. Leaders do.

The most effective organizations I've worked with have one thing in common: a culture of encouragement. Not false cheer. Not hype. Just leaders at every level speaking life into others—naming potential, celebrating progress, and anchoring people in their own worth.

In psychology, this idea is supported by the Pygmalion effect — the concept that people tend to rise or fall to the expectations set for them. When leaders expect the best and consistently communicate that belief, people often meet those expectations (Rosenthal & Jacobson, 1968).

FINAL THOUGHT: BE REMEMBERED FOR THE RIGHT WORDS

I'll leave you with this.

The words you speak as a leader don't just drift into the air. They settle. Sometimes softly. Sometimes like a lifeline. Sometimes like the first sunlight after a long night.

When you tell someone you see greatness in them, even when they doubt themselves—especially when they doubt themselves—you're doing more than just motivating. You're affirming them. You're providing a perspective that helps them start to see themselves differently.

And they don't forget that.

So, speak life. Speak it often. Speak it with care.

Be the kind of leader whose words are remembered when the lights are dim, the pressure's intense, and someone questions if they have what it takes.

Because they do.

And you just might be the one who helps them see it.

TEAM APPLICATION

Create a "shout-out" section during team meetings.

Rotate the Encourager role during projects.

Ask each person, "Who encouraged you this month, and why did it matter?"

LEADER'S JOURNAL

When was the last time I told someone, "I see greatness in you"?

TEAM CHALLENGE

This month, encourage your team to "catch someone doing something right" and share it aloud or in writing.

LEADERSHIP REFLECTION

Who on my team needs encouragement right now-and what's one specific thing I can affirm in them?

ONE-LINER TO REMEMBER

"Encouragement doesn't cost much, but it can change everything."

PART TWO
THE CHARACTER OF A LEADER

CHAPTER 5
ACCOUNTABILITY – OWNING THE WORK AND THE OUTCOME

I'VE ENTERED countless organizations filled with talented people and brilliant strategies—yet accountability is often missing like a cracked foundation beneath a skyscraper. No matter how well-intentioned a vision is, it can't stand tall on charisma alone. Accountability is what gives weight to our words and trust to our teams. Without it, the best plans fall apart into excuses, and the most promising teams splinter under the strain of uncertainty.

LEADERSHIP SNAPSHOT:

When Satya Nadella became CEO of Microsoft, he shifted the company's culture from a "know-it-all" to a "learn-it-all" mindset. By demonstrating accountability and taking responsibility for both successes and failures, he encouraged curiosity, transparency, and growth. The result? Microsoft tripled its product innovation cycles and boosted employee retention by 40%.

OPENING THOUGHT

Leadership without accountability is simply authority.

True leaders don't just set expectations—they take ownership of the results, demonstrate the standard, and foster a culture where everyone is responsible for the work and the outcome.

WHY ACCOUNTABILITY MATTERS AS A LEADER

I learned early in my leadership journey that accountability isn't about catching people doing something wrong—it's about fostering an environment where people can do things right.

It's the quiet force behind every high-performing culture. It doesn't make headlines or trend on social media, but it's the reason communication flows, trust deepens, and people feel safe enough to take meaningful risks. When accountability exists, teams move faster, innovation happens naturally, and people rely on each other.

But when it's absent, everything begins to fall apart. Outcomes become uncertain. Blame replaces accountability. People start protecting themselves instead of helping each other, and the mission declines.

Accountability matters because it shows respect for people. It says, "You are capable, and your contribution is important." It encourages us to fully engage for ourselves, for each other, and for the work we've committed to do.

As leaders, our willingness to model accountability sets the tone for everyone around us. It's one of the most powerful ways we build trust—and it's one of the greatest gifts we can give to those we lead.

The data supports this: a 2023 report by the Workplace Accountability Study found that organizations with strong cultures of accountability experience 30% higher innovation rates and 46% greater employee engagement. Gallup agrees, noting that engaged employees are more likely to stay with their companies and produce higher-quality work.

USING ACCOUNTABILITY TO GROW MY BUSINESS AND LEAD A HIGH-PERFORMING TEAM

When I first started my business, I wanted to create a space where people felt valued, trusted, and inspired to do their best work. I believed in people and in giving them freedom. But I soon realized that without accountability, freedom can lead to confusion.

There was a time when our business was growing, but we kept hitting the same walls: projects missed deadlines, small details slipped through the cracks, and I found myself taking on more and more of the workload just to keep things moving. I remember sitting at my desk late one evening thinking, "I can't keep doing it all myself."

That was the moment I realized that accountability isn't about controlling people—it's about caring enough to expect their best while giving them the support to achieve it.

I gathered the team and shared a new commitment: We would set clear weekly goals and check in every Friday. Not to catch mistakes, but to celebrate wins, address roadblocks early, and learn together. I told them, "We're all capable of greatness, and part of my job is to help us get there—together."

Initially, the team was quiet and unsure of what to expect. However, as the weeks went on, a change occurred. People began coming prepared, eager to share their progress and openly discuss challenges. They started collaborating to solve problems instead of working in isolation. They took ownership of their roles and took pride in fulfilling their commitments.

Accountability became our culture, not through fear but through a shared commitment to excellence. It freed me to lead instead of constantly putting out fires. It empowered my team to grow, and it allowed us to serve our clients with consistency and integrity.

Within a year, we saw our business grow, our client satisfaction improve, and our team members realize their potent potential in ways I couldn't have scripted.

This experience taught me that accountability is an act of love in leadership. It says to your people, "You matter. Your work matters. I see you, and I won't let you settle for less than your best." It turns potent potential into performance and transforms a business from good intentions into real, sustainable impact.

But let's be clear—accountability isn't about punishment or micromanagement. It's not a club you swing when things go wrong. It's a compass you carry to know your direction, and a mirror you hold to see who's responsible. It's about learning. It's about growth. And above all, it's about trust.

WHAT THIS IS (AND ISN'T)

I've observed leaders confuse accountability with control. They believe that by monitoring closely enough, no one will make a mistake. But that's oversight, not ownership.

Real accountability means owning both successes and failures, whether in public or private. It's about fostering clarity and consistent action—not enforcing compliance through fear.

When I worked with a retail leadership team struggling with turnover, their managers complained that employees weren't "taking initiative." But when we examined their communication practices, the real issue wasn't the employees—it was the lack of clear expectations and meaningful feedback. When people don't know what success looks like, they can't be held accountable for achieving it. Accountability without clarity is just chaos with consequences.

And here's what it definitely isn't: perfection. Being accountable doesn't mean never making mistakes; it means owning them, learning from them, and modeling that behavior for your team. One of the best things a leader can say is, "That was on me."

WHAT IT LOOKS LIKE

In healthy, accountable cultures, you see leaders doing things that are simple—but rare.

- They set clear, measurable expectations and confirm mutual understanding.
- They follow up—not with suspicion, but with support.
- They model the behaviors and standards they want to see.
- They own the mistakes and share the wins.
- They coach performance, helping team members get better rather than just pointing out what went wrong.

That's why accountability matters, and it's one of the best gifts you can give to your team—and yourself—as a leader.

WHAT HAPPENS WITHOUT IT

In the absence of accountability, organizations begin to unravel.

- Excuses take the place of action.
- Finger-pointing becomes the default response to every problem.
- Innovation stalls because no one wants to risk failure if they think they'll be scapegoated.
- Trust and morale deteriorate, creating disengagement and, ultimately, turnover.

When I supported a tech startup a few years ago, they were losing developers rapidly. Exit interviews revealed a common theme: "No one owns anything here." Projects were always delayed. Meetings were filled with vague promises. Deadlines were missed, but no one followed up on them. Accountability was so weak that it practically disappeared. After we set clear expectations, established transparent workflows, and introduced a simple yet regular check-in system, they began to see improvements—not just in meeting deadlines, but also in team energy.

HOW TO BUILD IT

So how do we build accountability into the DNA of our teams? Here are some proven practices:

1. SET CRYSTAL-CLEAR EXPECTATIONS

You can't hold people accountable for what they don't understand. Every role, project, and deliverable should come with unambiguous expectations. That includes defining what success looks like and how progress will be measured.
Use tools like SMART goals—Specific, Measurable, Achievable, Relevant, Time-bound—to eliminate guesswork. Clarity creates confidence, and confidence empowers ownership.

2. FOLLOW THROUGH

Accountability isn't a one-time agreement. It's a rhythm. Consistently following up—whether through one-on-ones, status reports, or team check-ins—shows that you care about the outcomes and the person behind them.
When leaders fail to follow up, it sends an unintended message: "This isn't important." But when you circle back consistently, you reinforce both responsibility and respect.

3. MODEL OWNERSHIP

If you want others to be accountable, you must set an example. This involves admitting your mistakes, seeking feedback, and making your commitments clear.

Psychologist Albert Bandura's social learning theory affirms what we already intuitively understand: people learn more from our actions than from our words. As a leader, your sense of ownership sets the tone.

4. GIVE TIMELY FEEDBACK

Don't wait for performance reviews or crises. Feedback should be immediate, actionable, and supportive. The goal isn't to scold but to build up.
Use the "SBI" model—Situation, Behavior, Impact—to make feedback more effective: "In today's meeting (Situation), you interrupted the client multiple times (Behavior), which made us seem unprepared (Impact). Let's work on letting them finish next time."

5. REWARD ACCOUNTABILITY

Catch people doing it right. When someone steps up, owns a mistake, or follows through with excellence—recognize it. Public acknowledgment reinforces the behavior you want to see repeated.
At one manufacturing company I worked with, a simple "Accountability Spotlight" at weekly team meetings transformed everything. Employees nominated colleagues who had taken responsibility in a meaningful way, and each recipient received a handwritten note from their manager. Engagement increased, and productivity improved.

THE 70-20-10 FRAMEWORK FOR BUILDING ACCOUNTABILITY

The 70-20-10 model, popularized in leadership development circles, is just as powerful when applied to building accountability:

- **70%** of accountability is learned on the job—through real responsibilities, stretch goals, and reflecting on results.
- **20%** comes from coaching and mentorship—the conversations where someone says, "Here's how you could do better," and actually helps you get there.
- **10%** is developed through formal training—courses, workshops, or playbooks that introduce tools and language around responsibility.

This means that if you want an accountable team, you can't just give them a handbook—you have to create opportunities for practice, reflection, and real-time feedback.

SITUATIONAL LEADERSHIP AND ACCOUNTABILITY

One framework I frequently use with clients is Situational Leadership, developed by Hersey and Blanchard. It emphasizes that effective leaders adapt their style based on the readiness of their team members—both in terms of skill and commitment.

When it comes to accountability:

- Novices need direction—what's expected, when, and how.
- Learners need coaching—support to keep growing while owning more.
- Capable but cautious employees need encouragement and space—to build confidence in their decisions.
- Experts need autonomy and trust—the freedom to deliver with minimal interference, but consistent support.

Accountability, then, is not a one-size-fits-all approach. It's responsive and relational. The leader's role is to help each person take ownership in a way that fits their current development level.

CASE IN POINT: THE MANUFACTURING PLANT THAT GOT IT RIGHT

One of my favorite examples of accountability in action comes from a story about a mid-sized manufacturing plant in the Midwest. The plant had struggled with costly production errors and declining morale. Leadership had been operating with a fear-based mindset—penalizing mistakes and over-monitoring every move.

Enter Rachel, a new plant manager with a different approach.

Instead of punishing mistakes, she introduced daily micro-teaching sessions and error analysis labs. Inspired by Carol Dweck's research on growth mindset, Rachel viewed errors as opportunities to improve systems, not just discipline individuals.

When a mistake occurred, her team asked three questions:

1. What was supposed to happen?
2. What actually happened?
3. What will we do differently next time?

This simple ritual normalized learning and removed shame. Within a year, production errors dropped by 62%, and employee satisfaction increased dramatically.

The difference? Accountability shifted from fear to ownership and growth.

FINAL THOUGHTS

Accountability isn't the most glamorous leadership trait—but it is, in my view, the most vital. Without it, trust diminishes, effort declines, and performance suffers. But with it? Teams thrive, individuals grow, and organizations realize their full potential.

So, let me ask you this: When the results come in—good or bad—do you take responsibility for them? Do you show your team what it means to be accountable, not just when it's easy, but when it really matters?

Because ultimately, accountability isn't a point you reach; it's a practice. It's the willingness to say, "I'm responsible," and the courage to live by it.

TEAM APPLICATION

- Ask: "What does true accountability look like on our team?"
- Celebrate examples of people owning outcomes, not just achieving results.
- Normalize accountability conversations, not just during performance reviews, but as a daily practice.
- Use OKRs (Objectives and Key Results) to set, track, and review shared goals for transparency and alignment.

LEADER'S JOURNAL

Where might I be tolerating avoidance or making excuses instead of promoting ownership and learning?

TEAM CHALLENGE

This quarter, ask your team to share an example of when they took ownership of a challenge and what they learned from it.

LEADERSHIP REFLECTION

How should I respond when things go wrong — do I look for someone to blame, or do I model accountability first?

ONE-LINER TO REMEMBER

"Accountability isn't about blame — it's about creating better outcomes, together."

CHAPTER 6
HUMILITY – STAYING GROUNDED WHILE REACHING HIGHER

YOU DON'T HAVE to know everything to lead well; you must stay coachable.

WHY THIS MATTERS

When I first started consulting, I believed success meant having all the answers. After all, wasn't that what clients paid for? Expertise. Confidence. Authority. But over time—and through a few tough lessons—I realized that what people value most is credibility, and credibility comes from humility, not bravado.

Humility is not weakness. It is not self-deprecation. In leadership, humility is one of the most potent sources of strength. It protects us from arrogance, which can sneak in subtly as we rise higher. It guards us from isolation, the dangerous trap where no one tells the emperor he has no clothes. And most importantly, humility keeps us learning. And learning leaders are the ones who last.

Jim Collins, in his landmark book Good to Great, describes Level 5 Leaders as those who combine deep personal humility with strong professional will. These leaders consistently outperform others—not because they are loud or flashy—but because they are grounded, open, and more focused on the mission than on themselves (Collins, 2001). I have seen this truth echoed repeatedly in the organizations I serve. The best leaders don't enter the room trying to prove they are the smartest—they enter trying to understand what they don't yet know.

Humility builds bridges, not silos. It opens conversations, encourages innovation, and fosters cultures where people feel safe to share. Without it, leadership becomes fragile. With it, leadership becomes transformative.

WHAT IT LOOKS LIKE

Let me share a few scenes from my experience.

A senior leader I once coached worked for a large commercial real estate company. You wouldn't guess it just by passing her on the street. She wore jeans to meetings, carried her own laptop, and often asked interns, "What would you do in my shoes?" Her humility wasn't for show; it was genuine. She understood that staying humble encouraged her team to speak up and share new ideas. Her team was the most engaged I've ever seen—scoring in the 95th percentile for voice and psychological safety.

Contrast that with another leader I worked with—a senior executive whose resume read like a who's who of global companies. He was brilliant, no doubt. But he didn't listen. He interrupted mid-sentence, assumed his opinion was the best, and rarely asked questions. Over time, his team disengaged. Talented individuals left. Innovation stalled. Why? Because no one likes to serve someone who's always right. Feedback dried up, and so did his results.

Humility looks like this:

- You admit mistakes quickly—without defensiveness or drama.
- You ask more questions than you answer—because you know you do not know everything.

- You listen actively—because others have wisdom you cannot afford to miss.
- You invite others to shine—because their success does not diminish yours.

Let me tell you, nothing boosts a team's confidence like a leader who doesn't seek the spotlight. I once advised a VP who made it a weekly practice to recognize one "unsung hero" in their department—someone who quietly solved a problem or supported a colleague without asking for applause. It transformed morale. People began looking for ways to contribute, not compete.

WHAT HAPPENS WITHOUT IT

If humility is oxygen, arrogance is like carbon monoxide—colorless, odorless, and ultimately deadly to your culture.

When leaders lack humility, leadership becomes disconnected. You start seeing what I call "executive insulation." Feedback is filtered. Truth becomes politicized. And gradually, good people stop speaking up not because they don't care, but because they believe it won't make a difference.

A Stanford study (Anderson, Brion, & Moore, 2012) found that power often reduces a person's ability to see things from others' perspectives. This "empathy erosion" can lead leaders to misinterpret situations and make poor choices—because they've lost the habit of truly listening.

In another company I worked with, a mid-level manager told me, "We used to give feedback in meetings. Now we just nod and wait for the storm to pass." That storm? A leader who confused dominance with direction. Within two years, turnover doubled. The culture hardened. People stopped trying to improve things because improvement wasn't welcome—it was seen as insubordination.

Humility serves as the remedy for this. It keeps your ears

open, your mind adaptable, and your heart connected with your people.

HOW TO BUILD IT

Let me be clear: humility isn't just a personality trait for experts and introverts. It's a practice—something any leader can develop intentionally. And here's how:

1. SHARE LEADERSHIP MISTAKES OPENLY.

Some of the most impactful moments I've experienced as a consultant occurred when I acknowledged my own blind spots. I once told a client I'd misunderstood a team dynamic—and my openness fostered a deeper conversation we might never have had if I had clung to my "expert" persona. Leaders who show vulnerability encourage others to be honest.
Try this: during your next team meeting, spend two minutes sharing a recent mistake and what you learned. It builds trust more quickly than any PowerPoint slide ever could.

2. ASK YOUR TEAM FOR ADVICE AND FEEDBACK.

This isn't just about "checking the box" with a suggestion form. I mean actively seeking feedback—asking questions like: "What am I missing?" or "What could we have done differently in that project?" and listening without defending.
Edgar Schein, the late organizational psychologist, coined the term humble inquiry—the art of asking instead of telling. It's not just good manners; it's a smart strategy. People support what they help create.

3. STAY CURIOUS ABOUT WHAT YOU DON'T KNOW.

In a world that changes as quickly as ours, leaders must continue to learn. Curiosity goes hand in hand with humility. I've worked with founders who built companies by asking three questions repeatedly: "What if?" "Why not?" and "How might we?"
One executive I coach sets a quarterly "ignorance goal"—a topic he knows little about that he commits to learning about. He encourages the team to do the same, and they share insights in an internal newsletter. That culture of learning? It began with a humble leader who wasn't afraid to admit he had more to learn.

4. CELEBRATE THE WINS WITHOUT TAKING ALL THE CREDIT.

Years ago, I facilitated a strategy retreat for a nonprofit that had just achieved a major milestone. The executive director stood up and said, "I didn't get us here. We got us here. And some of you carried more weight than I did." You could feel the pride in the room.
People prefer to work for leaders who genuinely appreciate them, rather than merely tolerate them.
Try this: In your next success debrief, focus more on highlighting others' contributions than your own. It shifts the energy from ego to ecosystem.

5. SHOW GENUINE INTEREST IN LEARNING FROM OTHERS.

Humility involves valuing every voice—not just those in leadership. I once shadowed a company president who routinely visited the customer service floor each week and asked, "What are customers telling you that we're not hearing in the boardroom?" He would take notes. He would follow up. Moreover, on more than one occasion, their most significant innovations originated from ideas conceived by frontline staff. That is the power of inclusive humility.

A FINAL STORY

Let me share a story that changed me.

Years ago, I was facilitating a leadership retreat for one of our clients. On the second day, a young, brilliant, and beloved-by-investors founder stood up during a session and said, "I need to apologize. I've been steamrolling our meetings. I haven't listened well. And if we're going to scale this company, I need to scale my humility."

Silence. Then applause. Followed by a flood of honest feedback, new ideas, and shared ownership that changed their direction. They went on to double their team, triple their revenue, and—most importantly—create a culture where humility wasn't just an aspiration. It was a way of being.

That's what's possible when leaders stay grounded while reaching higher.

TEAM APPLICATION

- Ask: "What's something you see that I might miss?"
- Share learning moments with your team.
- Invite different voices to lead discussions.

LEADERSHIP REFLECTION

When was the last time you said, "I don't know—but I'll find out"?

ONE-LINER TO REMEMBER

"Humility isn't losing yourself—it's not making it about yourself.

CHAPTER 7
SERVANT LEADERSHIP – PUTTING PEOPLE FIRST TO BUILD LASTING IMPACT

LEADERSHIP SNAPSHOT:

When Cheryl Bachelder became CEO of Popeyes Louisiana Kitchen, she shifted the company's focus from top-down directives to servant leadership. Popeyes experienced a 45% increase in profits and a significant rise in employee engagement and trust by prioritizing franchisee success and frontline empowerment. Bachelder's philosophy: "Leaders must serve those they lead, not the other way around."
(Bachelder, 2015; Greenleaf Center for Servant Leadership)

OPENING THOUGHT

If leadership is about you, it's not leadership.
Real leaders serve first.

WHY THIS MATTERS

There's a quote I share every time I facilitate a leadership workshop: "People Always Matter." It sounds simple, but it is profoundly true. I have seen talented strategists struggle in leadership roles because they focused more on control than on care, and on results rather than respect. Furthermore, I have seen quiet, behind-the-scenes leaders transform entire organizations simply by choosing to prioritize serving their people.

Servant leadership is more than just a feel-good philosophy; it is a practical, results-driven approach to building organizations where individuals are motivated to perform at their best. According to van Dierendonck (2011), servant leadership is positively associated with increased engagement, trust, and team effectiveness. Gallup's 2023 State of the Workplace Report further confirms that teams led by servant-oriented leaders are more collaborative and resilient, and they experience significantly lower turnover rates.

In my consulting career, I've worked with fast-growing startups, experienced Fortune 500 companies, and everything in between. The one consistent factor? Teams thrive when leaders focus on people.

When leaders serve and care for people, organizations prosper. When ego takes over, people and cultures become fractured.

WHAT THIS IS (AND ISN'T)

Let me clarify what servant leadership truly is—because too often, people confuse it with gentle leadership or avoiding tough decisions.

Servant leadership focuses on the needs, growth, and well-being of others. That doesn't mean you're weak. It doesn't mean you ignore performance, accountability, or strategic outcomes. It means you recognize that your role is to enable others to reach their full potential.

This isn't about being passive. In fact, servant leaders often have to make some of the toughest decisions—just from a different perspective. Instead of asking, "How does this serve me or my agenda?" the servant leader asks, "How does this decision serve our people, our mission, and our future?"

IMPACT LEADERSHIP   57

Robert K. Greenleaf, who first introduced the idea of servant leadership in 1977, described it as a leadership style that starts with a natural desire to serve. Only after addressing others' needs does the leader decide on direction and authority. It's about stewardship, not ownership.

Servant leaders don't hoard power—they empower and uplift others. They don't dominate meetings—they foster space for others. They don't micromanage—they trust, support, and coach.

SERVANT LEADERSHIP DURING CHAOS

There was a time in my career when I was asked to help a senior spiritual leader guide his entire organization through a period of significant, necessary change. This leader was highly respected—he had supported families through life and loss, built trust across generations, and was the kind of leader whose presence alone could bring calm to a room.

However, this was different.

The organization stood at a crossroads. It was clear that without significant shifts—in operations, finances, and culture—they would not stay relevant or sustainable for the next generation they serve. The necessary changes were not small adjustments; they involved letting go of long-standing traditions, realigning staff, and facing the fact that what had worked for decades was no longer effective.

This leader understood the changes were necessary, but he also recognized they would face resistance, grief, and misunderstanding. And he was not assured that his track record alone would be enough to see him through. This was going to be about servant leadership during the storm.

When I approached him, I didn't see a leader trying to hold onto his power. I saw a servant leader asking, "What does the organization need, and how do I steward this moment well, even if it costs me personally?"

He dedicated countless hours meeting with staff, board

members, and congregants, not to dictate their actions, but to listen deeply to their fears, hopes, and concerns. I observed him ask in meetings, "What is in your way right now?" and "What would it take for you to trust this process?" He spent more time removing barriers and clarifying confusion than enforcing decisions.

During a crucial meeting, when tensions were high and voices were raised, he stayed calm, recognizing the discomfort in the room while standing firm on what needed to change. Later, I asked him how he remained grounded in the chaos, and he quietly told me, "This isn't about me. It's about what God is calling us to be next, not what we're comfortable with now."

Gradually, through numerous one-on-one conversations and courageous moments of transparency, the organization began to change. Programs were adjusted, staff roles were clarified, and traditions were honored while making room for new practices to meet the evolving needs of the community. The leader credited others along the way, celebrating small wins and reminding the team why the work mattered.

It wasn't easy. Some people left, and some days felt heavy. But he never stopped showing up with humility, clarity, and care.

Watching him lead during that season changed me. It taught me that servant leadership isn't soft. It's sacrificial. It's the willingness to hold space for people's grief while still guiding them toward what is needed for the future. It's the courage to stay focused on the mission when it would be easier to keep people comfortable. And it's the quiet strength to say, "I will walk through this with you," even when the path is steep and uncertain.

This experience reminded me why I do this work: to help leaders lead with heart, even in chaos, and to help organizations shift from survival to significance while honoring people along the way.

That's an example of servant leadership in action.

Here's what it often looks like on the ground:

- You remove barriers so others can do their best work.
- You don't just give directions — you clear the way.
- You coach, support, and uplift—especially when it's inconvenient.
- When someone underperforms, you do not shame them. You ask what support they need to rise.
- You prioritize people over processes and policies.
- Bureaucracy serves the mission, not the other way around.
- You see leadership as a duty to serve, not a privilege to rule.

You lead because you owe something to the people you support—not because you're entitled to authority.

WHAT HAPPENS WITHOUT IT

Unfortunately, I have also seen what happens when it is absent.

At one organization—a tech services firm—leadership became more hierarchical. Commands moved in one direction. Meetings were dominated by executives more focused on being heard than listening. Performance reviews followed strict processes, ignoring real-time feedback from peers or clients.

Slowly but surely, the signs of decay crept in:

- Ego took center stage. Leaders prioritized their agendas over team input.
- Trust eroded. People hesitated to speak up or challenge decisions.
- Psychological safety disappeared. Innovation slowed. Fear grew.
- Turnover rose. High-potent [suggested: powerful]ial talent began to exit quietly.
- Organizational values collapsed under pressure. What

looked good on the website no longer matched the daily experience.

Eva et al. (2019) found that servant leadership is strongly connected to trust, team cohesion, and psychological safety. Remove it, and these elements decline significantly. Without servant leadership, teams become transactional. Leaders become disconnected. And culture turns into a buzzword instead of a lived experience.

HOW TO BUILD IT

The good news? Servant leadership can be cultivated—one conversation, one habit, and one mindset shift at a time. Here's what I've found most effective in practice:

1. *Ask before assuming: "How can I help?"—and listen for the real answer.*
Too many leaders assume they know what their team needs. Servant leaders *ask*. They create space for candid feedback, even if it's uncomfortable.

2. *Measure success by team growth, not personal praise.*
If your people are learning, contributing more, and stepping into leadership themselves, *you* are winning.

3. *Elevate others publicly.*
Recognition is rocket fuel. Spotlight the quiet contributors. Celebrate collaboration. Make others feel seen.

4. *Protect your team's ability to do their best work.*
This might mean pushing back on unrealistic timelines or shielding the team from reactive decisions. It's about advocating for what truly matters.

5. *Let people lead without micromanagement.*
Delegate real authority. Let others own decisions. Be there as a coach, not a controller.

CASE-IN-POINT

A few years ago, I was brought in to advise at a hospital system that was going through major changes—new leadership, new technologies, and serious budget pressures. The department I was working with had been struggling: morale was low, patient satisfaction was dropping, and turnover was rising.

The department head could have issued new mandates, enforced stricter protocols, or doubled down on performance metrics. Instead, she chose to listen.

She scheduled a series of 1:1 listening sessions and small-group discussions. In each one, she began with a simple question: "What's getting in the way of your best work?" Then she listened. And she took action.

She simplified burdensome documentation procedures. She advocated for more staffing resources. She recognized individuals who consistently went above and beyond—quietly and steadily. She held debriefs not only when things went wrong but also when things went right, so the team could learn and replicate success.

Within a year, patient satisfaction increased by 28%. Staff engagement scores jumped. And perhaps most importantly, people wanted to stay—not because of a retention bonus, but because they felt seen, valued, and supported.

Her legacy? Not just operational improvement—but a culture of dignity.

FINAL THOUGHT: LEAD LIKE A GARDENER

One of my favorite metaphors for impact leadership comes from the natural world. A gardener does not grow the plant. The plant grows itself—*if* the soil is rich, the conditions are right, and harmful weeds are kept at bay.

Servant leaders are gardeners. They don't control outcomes—they cultivate conditions. They don't aim to be the tallest tree—they make room for others to grow. They nourish the roots.

In every room I walk into, I remind myself: I'm not here to impress; I'm here to serve. That shift—from focusing on myself to caring for others—is where true leadership starts.

So, the next time you face a leadership challenge, pause and ask: "What would a servant leader do?" More often than not, the answer is simple, but not easy.

Listen. Uplift. Clear the way. And let others shine.

That is how lasting impact is built.

TEAM APPLICATION

- Ask: "Where can I better serve you or the team?"
- Reward and recognize servant leadership behaviors in your culture, not just results, but the way results are achieved.
- Build mentorship and peer support into your leadership pipeline.

LEADER'S JOURNAL

Am I building others-or building my own platform?

TEAM CHALLENGE

Invite team members to nominate a "servant leader of the month." Celebrate the person who best exemplifies putting others first.

LEADERSHIP REFLECTION

Where do I need to step back and let others lead?
What's one barrier I can remove for my team this week?

ONE-LINER TO REMEMBER

"Servant leadership builds the kind of teams people want to join-and stay with."

CHAPTER 8
LISTENER – THE MOST UNDERRATED LEADERSHIP SKILL

LEADERSHIP SNAPSHOT:

When Doug Conant became CEO of Campbell Soup Company, he wrote over 30,000 handwritten notes to employees, made a point to walk the halls daily, ask open-ended questions, and truly listen. This commitment to listening transformed Campbell's culture, reversing years of decline and restoring trust and engagement across the organization (Conant, 2011).

OPENING THOUGHT

Listening is not just a soft skill; it's the most essential skill of a leader. You can't lead people if you don't hear them, can't hear, or refuse to listen. Genuine listening transforms information into insight, and insight into action. It's remarkable that the words 'listen' and 'silent' share the same letters, which suggests that to listen effectively, I must be silent. This means slowing down our inner thoughts and being fully present when listening. I'm not talking about listening to respond, defend myself, or fix everything for everyone. I'm referring to the kind of listening that gives people the grace and space to be heard without judgment or interruption.

WHY THIS MATTERS

Over the years as a business leader, I've learned that most leaders significantly overestimate their listening skills. In fact, research shows we remember only about 25% of what we hear (Brownell, 2012). This troubling fact often surprises executives when I mention it in workshops, but it highlights why active listening isn't just helpful—it's essential.

Why does this really matter? In the fast-paced, ever-changing business world, leaders are conditioned and expected to speak, persuade, and decide swiftly and clearly. Yet listening, arguably the most underrated of leadership skills, forms the very foundation of accountability, trust, respect, and innovation. I've seen firsthand how organizations transform when leaders truly learn to listen. Teams led by genuinely attentive leaders report higher engagement, improved problem-solving skills, and notably stronger interpersonal relationships, as documented extensively by Harvard Business Review in 2016.

CONNECTING THROUGH LISTENING IN A FAST-PACED WORLD

Not long ago, I faced a leadership challenge that felt more personal than any boardroom or workshop: connecting with my teenager in a world of constant scrolling, buzzing notifications, and fast-paced distractions.

We were falling into a pattern I didn't like. Conversations felt one-sided, with me asking questions while she glanced down at her phone, replying with quick "yeah" or "I dunno." I could feel the distance growing, but I didn't know how to connect better with her while loving her.

One evening, after another brief, disconnected conversation, I realized something important: I wasn't really *listening* either. I was rushing through questions, expecting instant answers, and pushing for quick compliance instead of connection. I was *hearing* my teenager's words but not truly listening to her heart.

That night, I chose to try something new.

I asked her to meet me on the patio and invited her to put her phone down. I also put mine away. I told her, "I want to listen—not just to what you say, but to what matters to you." I love her unconditionally, and I wanted her to feel that, see that, hear that even when we see things differently.

Initially, there was silence—the kind that makes you want to fill the air with your own words. But I held back. Gradually, she began sharing, starting with short sentences, then moving on to stories about pressures at school, what it's like to feel the constant pull of notifications, and how difficult it is to keep up with everyone's highlight reels online.

As she spoke, I didn't correct, interrupt, or jump in to fix it. I just listened, nodded, and let her see that I was fully present. I asked, "How does that feel for you?" and "What do you need from me right now?" instead of lecturing on what she should or shouldn't do.

When it was my turn, I shared that I wasn't trying to control her or make her do what I would do if I were her; I wanted to understand what life felt like in her world, and I wanted us to have a healthy relationship, even as she was growing up.

That conversation changed something between us. It didn't magically erase the phone, the distractions, or the pace of the world. But it created a space where we could honestly talk, and she felt seen, heard, and valued.

In the weeks that followed, I noticed she began coming to me with questions and stories without being prompted. We found moments—over dinner, while driving, or before bed—where we would talk without distractions, even if just for five minutes. We laughed more, shared more, and the connection deepened.

This experience reminded me that leadership is about listening first. It's about slowing down in a fast-paced world to hear the unspoken concerns and dreams behind quick answers. It's about choosing connection over control, presence over productivity, and understanding over assumptions.

In a world where everyone has something to say and few really listen, choosing to listen to connect can be the greatest gift—and the most powerful leadership tool we have is being silent and being fully present while listening.

WHAT THIS IS (AND ISN'T)

Listening, genuine listening, goes well beyond simply processing spoken words. It involves understanding intent, emotion, and context. It's not about patiently waiting for your turn to speak or mentally rehearsing your response while someone else talks. It's active, intentional, respectful curiosity. Real listeners give their full attention, devices down, eyes up. They are fully present, asking clarifying questions and paraphrasing statements to confirm understanding.

WHAT IT LOOKS LIKE

As a parent, you decide to improve how you connect with your teenager, who is counting on you. You notice that every conversation feels rushed, with them distracted by constant phone notifications and quick one-word responses. Instead of demanding answers or giving lectures, you choose to slow down, put your own phone away, and say, "I want to hear you."

During conversations, you paid more attention to words than just words. You observed body language, the pauses before responses, and the subtle tone shifts that revealed what was really happening beneath the surface. When tensions around school or friendships came up, you could gently ask, "What's going on in your world that you wish I understood better?"

Those questions opened doors. The teenager, who often kept

feelings hidden, started to share stories about pressure at school, the stress of social media, and the fear of falling behind. Instead of shutting down, she felt seen and valued, and the relationship between my daughter and me has improved, and it's even fun at times.

Contrast this with what happens when we lead without listening. I've seen parents, often with good intentions, multitasking during conversations—checking emails, scrolling, or half-listening while giving advice. People often feel unheard and unimportant when their thoughts are dismissed in favor of quick solutions rather than real understanding. Over time, the relationship drifts, and conversations shrink to the bare minimum as trust quietly erodes.

Connection grows when we listen to understand, not just to respond. Whether at home or work, slowing down, removing distractions, and truly hearing what others are saying—and not saying—transforms conversations and relationships, laying a foundation for trust, growth, and genuine connection.

WHAT HAPPENS WITHOUT IT

Without active listening, misunderstandings grow. Problems stay unspoken, simmering quietly until they blow up. Talented employees leave, frustrated by their invisibility. And innovation? It completely stalls because collaboration of thought—the core of creativity—is held back.

HOW TO BUILD IT

Building a strong listening culture isn't just possible; it's easy with practice. The first technique I always teach leaders is active listening. Paraphrase what you've heard before you respond. It's deceptively simple, yet incredibly powerful. I remember teaching this approach to a leadership team at a company struggling with employee disputes. Within weeks, their conversations changed.

Employees said they felt truly heard for the first time, and tensions decreased significantly.

The second technique involves embracing silence. Leaders often rush to fill conversational gaps, believing that silence indicates confusion or a lack of agreement. Instead, I encourage clients to pause intentionally before replying, allowing others to elaborate further. "Tell me more," or "What's your perspective?" are simple, open-ended questions that invite deeper dialogue.

A study published in the Journal of Applied Psychology underscores the importance of emotional listening—recognizing feelings beneath words. When a leader acknowledges emotional undertones—such as frustration, anxiety, and excitement—employees feel profoundly valued and understood. This emotional resonance strengthens bonds and encourages candid communication.

Lastly, true listening requires humility. Inviting feedback on your listening skills is critical. Simply asking your team, "Do you feel heard by me?" opens the door to transparency and improvement. I once worked with an executive team whose members habitually interrupted each other. After introducing this reflective practice, their interactions improved dramatically, with tangible benefits to collaboration and productivity.

Listening is indeed a quietly revolutionary skill. It fosters trust, cultivates innovation, and enriches human connections. It moves leaders beyond transactional interactions to transformational relationships, empowering their teams to contribute fully and fearlessly.

As you lead, ask yourself regularly: Am I truly listening? It might just be the most important question you have ever asked.

CASE-IN-POINT

Donna, an experienced project manager, noticed that her usually lively team was becoming more disengaged. During meetings, conversations had become dull, ideas were few, and the energetic exchanges she once valued had mostly disappeared. The normally cooperative group had turned passive, often just nodding along to her instructions without offering meaningful input or enthusiasm. Donna sensed something was wrong, but despite her efforts to ask for feedback openly, no one shared their concerns.

Realizing that the usual group dynamic had become a barrier rather than a facilitator for open communication, Donna decided to change her approach. She started scheduling private, one-on-one listening sessions with each team member, framing these conversations as safe spaces entirely dedicated to their voices. She regularly asked a straightforward yet powerful question: "What's working—and what's not?" This open-ended method encouraged honesty and vulnerability, assuring her team that their perspectives were truly valued.

As she engaged deeply and attentively, actively listening without jumping to solutions or defenses, Donna uncovered a mosaic of minor frustrations that had quietly eroded team morale. For some, it was logistical hurdles like unnecessary administrative processes that wasted valuable time. For others, it was interpersonal tensions or feeling undervalued for their contributions. None of these issues were particularly significant on their own, but together, they created noticeable friction and dissatisfaction within the team.

By systematically addressing these concerns, Donna made targeted improvements: streamlining burdensome procedures, improving communication channels, and openly recognizing individual contributions in team meetings. The impact was quick and significant. Within weeks, engagement increased by 30%, and a renewed sense of collective purpose developed. Team members who had once been silent in meetings now eagerly shared new ideas, sparking innovations that had previously seemed unreachable.

Donna learned an important leadership lesson from this experience: her team didn't need more directives, new policies, or motivational speeches—they needed to feel heard, seen, and valued. Effective listening became the key to transformation, ultimately boosting the team's spirit and productivity.

TEAM APPLICATION

- Begin meetings with a "listening round"-everyone shares without interruption.
- Assign a "listener" role in discussions to capture key points and emotions.
- Regularly ask, "What's something we might be missing?" to surface hidden insights.

LEADER'S JOURNAL

When was the last time I listened without interrupting or judging?
What did I learn that surprised me?

TEAM CHALLENGE

This week, challenge your team to practice "no-interruption" listening in one meeting. Debrief: How did it feel? What did you notice?

LEADERSHIP REFLECTION

Who on my team might be waiting to be heard?
How can I make more space for their voice?

ONE-LINER TO REMEMBER

"Listening is the shortest path to trust, and the surest way to lead."

PART THREE
THE COURAGE TO LEAD

CHAPTER 9
COURAGE – STANDING STRONG IN THE FACE OF ADVERSITY

LEADERSHIP SNAPSHOT:

IN 1962, Rachel Carson published Silent Spring, a groundbreaking exposé on the environmental impacts of pesticides. Immediately, she faced intense backlash from powerful chemical corporations aimed at discrediting her. Despite being labeled alarmist, anti-progress, and unscientific, Carson remained unwavering. Her steadfast courage sparked widespread public awareness, legislative changes, and ultimately, the birth of the modern environmental movement. Carson's bravery didn't just change environmental policy; it demonstrated that one leader's courage can truly reshape the world.

OPENING THOUGHT:

Over my years of working with leaders across different industries, one truth becomes clear: effective leadership requires courageous action, not just safe choices. Courage is that powerful force that propels teams forward, even when fear, risk, or resistance try to hold them back.

WHY THIS MATTERS:

In the realm of leadership skills, courage is the most important—truly the foundation of all skills. On my leadership journey, I've repeatedly seen that courage separates good leaders from exceptional ones, especially during crises, uncertainty, or major change.

Research consistently highlights this. Courageous leaders not only motivate higher performance but also create an environment conducive to innovation and psychological safety. According to Brené Brown's extensive work on vulnerability and courage, leaders who embrace bravery cultivate resilient organizations where team members feel truly empowered to act courageously themselves (Brown 2018). Additionally, Harvard Business Review studies have confirmed that organizations led by courageous leaders consistently outperform their peers, especially during volatile periods (Harvard Business Review, 2019).

Now, more than ever, brave leadership is essential. To challenge outdated systems, handle complex crises, and build organizations that serve the broader societal good, courage must be a foundation, not optional.

WHAT THIS IS (AND ISN'T):

When I speak about courage in leadership workshops, I often clarify what courage truly entails.

Courage involves bold, values-driven action in the face of fear or adversity. It is not reckless bravado or impulsive risk-taking. Courage requires standing firmly for what's right, even if it is costly or unpopular. True courage recognizes fear but refuses to let it control you. It often shows up subtly, in quiet decisions and everyday acts, just as powerfully as in big, defining moments.

WHAT IT LOOKS LIKE:

In practice, courageous leadership often manifests in distinct behaviors I have observed repeatedly:

- Leaders who openly challenge ineffective, unjust, or outdated systems.
- Advocates who tirelessly champion their people, even when it creates friction or inconvenience.
- Individuals who willingly take unpopular stances guided by deep, self-transcendent values.
- Visionaries who step boldly into uncertain futures, balancing risk with ethical integrity.
- Facilitators who courageously initiate uncomfortable conversations, encouraging others to engage authentically.

WHAT HAPPENS WITHOUT IT:

In stark contrast, organizations lacking courageous leadership display unmistakable patterns of dysfunction:

- They become trapped by the status quo, mired in mediocrity and stagnation.
- Innovation is stifled by pervasive risk aversion and fear-driven paralysis.
- Problems remain unspoken, silently festering until crises inevitably erupt.
- Employee morale deteriorates, trust fractures, and disillusionment spreads.
- Teams grow passive, hesitant to act without explicit direction or permission, breeding a culture of dependence rather than initiative.

CASE-IN-POINT: LEADING WITH COURAGE WHEN THE WORLD SHUT DOWN

Let me share a real example from my experience. During the COVID-19 pandemic, as the world shut down and uncertainty spread through every household and organization, I worked with a leader navigating one of the toughest seasons of her career.

She led a community organization helping vulnerable families —many who lost jobs overnight, faced food insecurity, and were cut off from support networks. Meanwhile, her superiors demanded immediate budget cuts due to declining revenues, even if it meant eliminating programs that had become vital for people during the crisis.

She faced a tough choice: follow orders to cut services and keep her political position or stand up for the people she served and risk losing her job at a time when job security was uncertain for everyone.

She chose courage.

Instead of retreating, she gathered data, stories from families, and projections showing how cuts would worsen the community's crisis. She built alliances across departments, worked long hours to find creative savings elsewhere, and presented a clear, compelling case that protecting essential services would prevent long-term harm that would be much more costly to fix later.

Some in leadership were frustrated with her resistance, and she knew she was putting her own position at risk. But she also knew what mattered most.

Her courage wasn't loud or dramatic. It appeared in late-night Zoom calls with staff, checking in to see how they were coping with their fears while still showing up for families in need. It manifested in quiet moments when she reassured her team that they would get through this together, even without all the answers. It was evident in her advocacy for clients who had no other voice during chaotic times.

In the end, although she temporarily lost favor with some superiors, her integrity remained intact. Her team's morale soared, knowing their leader was willing to stand up for what mattered. They worked together, found creative ways to keep serving families safely, and rediscovered a strong sense of purpose and unity.

This experience reminded me that courage in a crisis isn't about making noise—it's about standing firm for your values when it's easier to give in. It's about caring enough for your people and those you serve that you are willing to risk your own comfort and security to do what's right.

And often, it's in those moments of quiet courage, when the world is shut down and fear is loud, that the most powerful, lasting leadership impact is made.

HOW TO BUILD IT:

In consulting practice, I focus on practical steps to build courage. Here are actionable methods you can start using right away:

1. Identify the complicated conversation or decision you are avoiding: True courage begins with honest self-reflection. Recognizing what you fear allows proactive preparation and clarity.
2. Take a calculated risk this week: Courage is not impulsive. It involves thoughtfully weighing consequences and taking deliberate, bold actions despite uncertainty.
3. Speak up for someone overlooked or marginalized: Courage means using your voice as a tool for justice, inclusion, and amplifying those who need support.
4. Reframe fear as opportunity: Psychologists argue that reframing uncertainty as growth can significantly alter your response to fear, transforming it into a catalyst rather than a barrier (Dweck, 2006).
5. Lead change, even without guaranteed outcomes: Courageous

leaders act guided by vision and values, not merely assured outcomes. Embracing ambiguity is a cornerstone of courageous leadership.

6. Practice 'try, trust, and tell' courage:

- Try Courage: Take actionable steps even amid perceived risks.
- Trust Courage: Rely on others, empower teams, and foster mutual dependence.
- Tell Courage: Commit to speaking openly, clearly, and honestly, especially in difficult situations.

By actively fostering courage, leaders can transform their teams and organizations into thriving, resilient, and innovative communities ready to navigate the complexities of our rapidly changing world.

TEAM APPLICATION

- Ask: "Where do we need more courage as a team?"
- Recognize and celebrate small acts of bravery, not just big wins.
- Make it safe to try, fail, and grow. Create a culture where vulnerability and risk-taking are rewarded, not punished.
- Role-play tough conversations to build "tell courage" muscle.

LEADERSHIP REFLECTION

What would I do today if I was leading from courage, not fear? Where is my team waiting for me to go first?

TEAM CHALLENGE

Invite team members to share a recent moment when they acted with courage, and what they learned from it.

ONE-LINER TO REMEMBER

"Courage in leadership isn't loud-it's bold, values-driven, and contagious when it matters most."

CHAPTER 10
POISED – STAYING GROUNDED IN PRESSURE
THE POWER OF POISE IN LEADERSHIP

WE'VE ALL SEEN IT—A leader enters a tense room, and without saying a word, the atmosphere shifts. Shoulders relax. Breath becomes steady. People lean in, eager to listen and participate. That is the quiet, commanding power of poise.

True poise isn't about having all the answers or keeping a perfect exterior. It comes from deep self-awareness, emotional intelligence, and intentional practice. It happens in moments when we choose to pause before reacting, breathe before speaking, and stay grounded when everything around us seems to be spinning.

I learned the importance of poise when I was just 25 years old, leading Soldiers into combat during Desert Storm. I was young, and the reality of leading people into a situation where the risks were real and the uncertainty was constant weighed heavily on me. There were nights I lay awake, questioning whether I was ready, if I was making the right decisions, or if I could handle the weight of these lives entrusted to my leadership.

But when I stepped in front of my Soldiers, I knew they didn't need to see my fear; they needed to see my steadiness. They needed to believe that, together, we could face whatever came our way. I learned to take a deep breath before I spoke, to steady my voice even when my heart was pounding, and to make eye contact that communicated, "I am here with you and for you."

There was a moment, just before a mission, when one of my Soldiers pulled me aside, eyes wide with fear, and asked, "Sergeant, are we going to be okay?" In that instant, I felt all of my own uncertainty—and then I chose to stand tall. I placed a hand on his shoulder, looked him in the eyes, and said, "We're going to take it one step at a time, and we're going to take care of each other. We will get through this."

That moment was not about pretending I was not afraid; it was about leading through my fear so they could find courage in theirs.

Poise isn't about lacking fear or doubt; it's about the ability to lead ourselves first so we can lead others effectively. It's about choosing to respond instead of react, staying present in conversations instead of rushing to solutions, and holding space for others' emotions without becoming overwhelmed by them.

During times of uncertainty—and every leader will face them—poise becomes an invaluable asset. When others are anxious, a poised leader acts as a steady anchor, reminding the team that they are safe, seen, and capable of navigating the challenges ahead. It allows leaders to guide with grace, not just grit, and to model calm confidence that empowers others to bring their best selves forward.

In mastering poise, leaders don't just weather storms—they turn them into chances for growth and connection. They become the calm amid chaos, the quiet strength others draw courage from, and the example that teaches teams how to handle adversity with resilience and dignity.

Poise is not reserved for the select few; it is a skill we build daily. Every moment we choose curiosity over defensiveness, presence over distraction, and compassion over judgment, we strengthen our capacity to lead with poise.

And in a world that often feels hurried, reactive, and restless, leaders who embody true poise stand out—not because they seek attention, but because they inspire trust, even amid uncertainty.

LEADERSHIP SNAPSHOT

C. Delores Tucker, my cousin, was a powerful force whose influence is still felt today. As one of the first Black women to serve as Secretary of State in the United States, she faced constant scrutiny, opposition, and resistance—often just for daring to occupy space in rooms where women like her had long been kept out.

Still, she never let the weight of resistance silence her voice or shatter her spirit. She stayed firm in her beliefs, fueled by a deep sense of purpose rooted in her faith and dedication to justice. Whether advocating for civil rights, women's rights, or speaking out boldly against messages she believed harmed the next generation, she carried herself with poise and an unwavering presence that commanded attention — not for herself, but for the causes she supported.

Her poise wasn't passive. It was an active, disciplined choice to remain composed while speaking truth to power, even when it was unpopular. I remember watching her handle harsh criticism with a calm, confident smile, her eyes steady, her voice clear, reminding everyone in the room that the work was bigger than her comfort or reputation.

When chaos surrounded her, she became a steady anchor for others afraid to speak up. Her ability to stand firm under pressure inspired many young leaders, showing them that poise isn't about avoiding conflict but about holding your ground with grace, even when the storm rages.

C. Delores Tucker exemplified true leadership: unwavering presence during challenges, a strong dedication to values over fame, and a bravery that encourages others to stand taller and speak out more forcefully for what is right.

OPENING THOUGHT

Poise is the calm in the storm—inner strength that keeps you steady when the world watches and the stakes are high. It's not just an external show but a true reflection of inner harmony and self-control.

WHY THIS MATTERS

Poise distinguishes between reacting and responding—between fueling chaos and bringing clarity when it matters most. In leadership, people observe you closely, especially during crises or uncertain times. Whether you realize it or not, your team reflects your emotional state. If you stay calm, clear, and grounded, they feel secure enough to remain focused and steady. If you are reactive and scattered, they will be too.

A Harvard Business Review study found that 71 percent of employees trust leaders more when they stay calm during stressful situations. That's because poise fosters psychological safety. It signals to your team, "You are safe to think, question, try, and grow—even when things are tough." Poise helps your team focus on solutions instead of worrying about your emotional state or the potential fallout of mistakes.

In my work with leaders, I've observed how those who practice poise create environments where people feel encouraged to innovate, share honest feedback, and face challenges together. I've witnessed leaders walk into tense boardrooms with raised voices and frustration thick in the air, and with a single moment of pause —a breath, a steady tone, a calm question—they change the entire atmosphere. Their teams lean in instead of shutting down. Conversations open up rather than spiral into blame.

Poised leaders become anchors, stabilizing their teams so they can perform their best work under pressure. They recognize that their presence influences the emotional atmosphere of the room, whether that room is a conference table, a hospital floor, a combat zone, or a family dinner table. They learn to manage the tension of uncertainty while offering a vision of what is achievable, allowing others to step forward with confidence rather than fear.

Without poise, trust unravels quickly. Teams become hesitant, defensive, and cautious, afraid to speak up or take initiative—energy shifts from solving problems to managing stress and navigating unspoken tension. Meetings become arenas of caution instead of platforms for collaboration. Innovation dies in environments where people feel they must tread carefully.

Poise is not about pretending you aren't under pressure or suppressing your emotions. It's about leading yourself first so you can lead others well. It's about slowing down enough to choose a thoughtful response instead of a quick reaction. It's about being fully present in the moment, even when everything around you feels uncertain.

Poise says, "I am here, and I am with you." It is evident in your steady tone, open posture, and willingness to listen before speaking. It shows when you take a breath before answering a tricky question, pause to truly hear what's being said beneath the words, and extend grace while holding accountability.

This is why poise matters in leadership: it maintains your impact, safeguards your relationships, and enhances your ability to lead during times when people need it most. It is a gift to your team, your organization, and yourself, helping you handle challenges with confidence and clarity while inspiring others to do the same.

And in a world that often feels hurried, reactive, and restless, leaders who demonstrate poise stand out—not because they seek attention, but because they earn trust, even when uncertainty surrounds them.

WHAT THIS IS (AND ISN'T)

Poise is a subtle combination of emotional intelligence, deep self-awareness, and purposeful presence. It's not just about appearing calm; instead, it involves truly understanding your inner emotional state, which allows for thoughtful responses rather than impulsive reactions.

Poise is also different from passivity or detachment. It's an active, grounded form of leadership that offers clarity and stability to others. Leaders with poise are fully engaged, purposeful, and responsive — not distant observers.

WHAT IT LOOKS LIKE

As a consultant, I have coached leaders across various industries and noticed consistent behaviors that demonstrate poise.

- Steady body language and measured tone: Even under intense scrutiny, poised leaders keep open, calm physical gestures that reassure and stabilize their teams.
- Intentional pauses: They intentionally use short silences to carefully think about their responses instead of reacting impulsively.
- Clear and calm communication: Even in emotionally charged situations, poised leaders communicate their messages transparently and compassionately, reducing misunderstandings.
- Adaptability: They smoothly adjust to changing circumstances, keeping an internal balance that reassures their teams.
- Modeling resilience: By showing strength and confidence during tough times, poised leaders inspire similar resilience within their teams.

WHAT HAPPENS WITHOUT IT

The absence of poise can trigger severe organizational repercussions:

- Anxiety and tension: Stress rapidly permeates teams, eroding collaboration and creativity.
- Escalation of minor issues: Without poised leadership, small conflicts or problems can spiral uncontrollably, becoming crises.
- Erosion of trust: Leaders who react emotionally rather than respond thoughtfully erode trust, creating dysfunctional and unproductive teams.
- Erratic decision-making: Impulsive responses lead to poor decisions, inconsistent policies, and delayed resolutions.
- Mirroring stress: Teams reflect their leader's anxiety, leading to lower morale, diminished performance, and high attrition.

CASE-IN-POINT

I recall consulting for a Fortune 500 company where a senior executive received blunt, critical feedback about his cultural fit. Instead of reacting defensively, he calmly paused, sincerely thanked his colleagues for their openness, and asked for more time to thoughtfully consider the feedback. His composed response turned a potentially challenging situation into a key growth opportunity, greatly improving trust and openness within the leadership team. This executive's calmness was transformative, fostering a culture where constructive feedback was seen as normal rather than intimidating.

HOW TO BUILD IT

In my experience guiding business leaders through high-pressure situations, I've identified several effective strategies to develop poise.

1. Control Your Breathing
Use breathing techniques like the 4-7-8 method (inhale for four seconds, hold for seven, exhale for eight) to quickly calm your nervous system. Renowned psychologist Dr. Andrew Weil recommends this method for reducing stress, promoting clarity, and boosting overall resilience under pressure.

2. Ground Your Body Language
Nonverbal cues greatly impact perceptions of leadership poise. Stand or sit upright, keep your posture open, and hold steady eye contact. Research by social psychologist Amy Cuddy shows that "power poses" (open, expansive postures) can boost confidence and effectively lower stress hormones, fostering genuine composure.

3. Pause Before Responding
In emotionally charged situations, deliberately pause. Leaders often feel pressure to respond immediately, but composed leaders recognize the value of intentional silence. This pause creates the mental space needed to craft thoughtful, strategic responses instead of reacting emotionally.

4. Prepare for the Unexpected
Thorough preparation boosts confidence and calmness under pressure. Prepare for potential challenges by mentally rehearsing or simulating responses. Renowned leadership consultant Dr. Marshall Goldsmith highlights the importance of "scenario planning" in building strong leadership composure and readiness for any situation.

5. Regulate Your Emotions

Practicing mindfulness or engaging in regular reflective exercises can greatly improve emotional regulation. Psychologist Daniel Goleman, the foremost authority on emotional intelligence, highlights recognizing emotional triggers as key to maintaining intentional control. Developing emotional self-awareness enables leaders to respond intentionally, strengthening internal composure.

6. Practice Adaptability

Poise is closely connected to adaptability—the ability to handle change gracefully. Leaders who stubbornly stick to initial plans or expectations find it hard to stay composed. Being flexible, open to change, and proactive in adjusting help maintain internal balance, which is crucial for poised leadership.

TEAM APPLICATION

- Begin meetings with a grounding exercise, deep breaths, or a moment of stillness.
- Role-play challenging scenarios to practice poised responses.
- Debrief after high-pressure moments: "How did our composure affect the outcome?"
- Encourage feedback on how your presence impacts the team in stressful times.

LEADERSHIP REFLECTION

How do I show up when the pressure is high?
What habits help me stay grounded-and what triggers throw me off balance?

TEAM CHALLENGE

Invite your team to share one strategy they use to stay composed under stress, and commit to practicing one new technique together this month.

ONE-LINER TO REMEMBER

"Poise is not the absence of pressure-it's the presence of calm, clarity, and confidence when it matters most."

CHAPTER 11
PASSION – LEADING WITH FIRE, ENERGY, AND DETERMINATION

PASSION ISN'T OPTIONAL for great leadership—it's vital. It's the heartbeat that turns jobs into missions and teams into movements. Passionate leadership doesn't just meet goals; it exceeds them, inspiring innovation, dedication, and ongoing growth. By intentionally cultivating and showing passion, leaders not only build successful organizations but also create lasting, meaningful legacies.

OPENING THOUGHT

Without passion, leadership is merely preserving the status quo. With passion, leadership transforms into a movement that draws others in, shapes culture, and generates momentum that lasts beyond titles and positions.

Passion is the spark that turns a job into a mission, transforming obligations into opportunities and daily routines into meaningful work. It's the fire in your eyes when you talk about what matters most, the conviction in your voice that reminds people why they show up each day. It's what gets you out of bed on tough days and keeps you going when obstacles seem unending.

Passion is not just emotional fuel—it's magnetic. It energizes you, but more importantly, it energizes those around you. It spreads, lifting the atmosphere of an entire team or organization, reminding people that their contributions matter and that they are part of something bigger than themselves.

Over my years working with leaders from various fields — including corporate executives, nonprofit founders, and military commanders — I've repeatedly seen this truth: Passionate leaders stand out. They don't just finish tasks; they inspire belief in the mission. They don't just get compliance from their teams; they earn commitment, creativity, and loyalty. Their people don't just show up for a paycheck; they show up because they believe in the work and want to be part of it.

Passion clarifies leadership. When a leader's passion is clear, it breaks through distractions and constant demands. It directs focus to what truly matters, aligning people and resources with purpose instead of mere activity. It reminds teams why they face challenges and how their efforts matter.

Passion also sustains leaders during adversity. It becomes the anchor in times of uncertainty, the reason you keep leading when it would be easier to step back or settle for less. It helps you lead with energy and authenticity, even when you're tired, because you're connected to your "why."

But passion isn't loud just to be noisy. It's not about constant hype or superficial enthusiasm. It is a deep, steady flame that burns within leaders who are aligned with their purpose, who care profoundly about people, and who are willing to take risks for what they believe in. Passionate leaders bring courage to spaces where fear has taken hold, possibility where limits have been assumed, and hope where discouragement has settled.

And here's what I've learned: Passionate leadership isn't limited to a few extroverted individuals or those with dramatic life stories. It's a choice—an intentional effort to stay connected to your purpose and lead with conviction. It's developed in quiet moments of reflection, through courageous conversations, and in the consistent decision to show up fully, day after day.

Passion distinguishes leaders who simply finish projects from those who leave a lasting impact through lives changed, systems transformed, and people who improve because they were truly cared for.

If you want to create a lasting impact, let your leadership be driven by passion. Because when you lead with passion, you don't just lead—you inspire, you mobilize, and you make it possible for others to see what is possible when they, too, lead with purpose and heart.

WHY THIS MATTERS

Passion sustains energy, accelerates buy-in, and creates movements, not just missions. It transforms everyday tasks into meaningful contributions. When leaders are passionate, teams adopt that same enthusiasm. Harvard Business Review's extensive studies show that employee engagement increases significantly when leaders display genuine passion and excitement for their work. According to Gallup's annual workplace surveys, companies with highly engaged teams consistently outperform their competitors in profitability, productivity, and innovation.

Teams naturally reflect the energy their leaders project. If you enter a room filled with energy, passion, and determination, those around you will pick up on it. On the other hand, a leader who seems disinterested or just going through the motions will see that same lack of enthusiasm show in their team's performance.

WHAT IT LOOKS LIKE

You speak about the mission with genuine excitement.
I've worked with leaders who talk about their organization's mission as if it's a burden, something they reluctantly carry. In contrast,

leaders who speak with passion light up the room. They lean forward, their eyes sparkle, and they genuinely smile. Their language isn't transactional; it's transformative. Simon Sinek famously described this as finding your "why." When you communicate your mission passionately, people don't just hear—they feel the difference.

You pursue excellence because you believe it matters.
Passionate leaders aren't satisfied with just good enough; they pursue excellence because mediocrity conflicts with their core values. Excellence isn't about perfectionism—it's about striving and continually growing. One client, a hospital CEO I advised, refused to accept industry-standard care metrics. She strongly believed each patient deserved exceptional care. Her steadfast commitment led the hospital to earn national recognition for patient satisfaction and clinical outcomes.

You inspire others through your own investment.
When I was advising a public education leader facing rapid growth and severe burnout, his leader consistently showed his passion by personally dedicating time to mentoring young leaders. His genuine enthusiasm and direct involvement revealed a key truth: passion doesn't delegate from afar; it actively participates. His team saw his authenticity, mirrored his dedication, and rallied impressively, ultimately tripling their productivity.

You model joyful urgency—not frantic chaos.
True passion shows as joyful urgency instead of chaos caused by stress. Great leaders show urgency in pursuing important goals, but they stay clear and optimistic. A nonprofit director I worked with, who was focused on fatherhood, acted with strong determination—but always kept joy at the forefront. His cheerful push for quick action rallied donors, volunteers, and community partners alike, building sustainable and impactful programs.

WHAT HAPPENS WITHOUT IT

Teams check boxes instead of chasing impact.
When passion diminishes, tasks turn mechanical. Instead of striving for meaningful impact, teams merely check off boxes, going through the motions without true commitment. I've observed organizations stagnate when their leaders lose focus on the core of the mission. Work becomes a routine, lifeless and lacking innovation or enthusiasm.

Growth stagnates.
Passion fuels innovation and growth. Without it, creativity and risk-taking diminish, giving way to a cautious, step-by-step approach that eventually causes stagnation. Businesses lose their competitive edge. They become reactive, trailing behind rivals who passionately pursue their mission.

Disengagement spreads.
Employee disengagement often reflects leadership passion—or the lack of it. A disengaged leader sends subtle yet powerful signals that the work is just functional, not meaningful. According to Gallup, disengaged teams experience lower productivity, higher turnover, and decreased morale. I have seen companies fail because leaders lost their passion and, along with it, their ability to inspire.

Innovation dims.
Innovation relies on passion. Without passionate leadership, ideas remain unspoken and unrealized. A manufacturing company I advised struggled to innovate because its leadership team put compliance and control above creativity. When passion faded, innovation stopped, leading to a steady decline until a passionate leader revived their culture, reigniting creativity and growth.

HOW TO BUILD IT

1. Reconnect to your purpose regularly.
Passion can diminish without deliberate effort. Regularly revisit your purpose—your "why." Journal it, speak it aloud, and remind yourself why your work matters. According to psychologist Mihaly Csikszentmihalyi, reconnecting with core purposes and aligning them with daily tasks consistently promotes flow and passionate engagement.

2. Share stories that reignite meaning.
Stories are powerful tools. They reconnect teams to the true meaning behind their work. As consultant Patrick Lencioni advises, leaders must consistently share compelling stories that emphasize the impact and importance of their organization's mission. In my practice, I encourage leaders to celebrate real-life examples where their mission has made tangible differences.

3. Protect the work that energizes you—not just drains you.
Leaders often see their passion fade because of tasks that drain rather than energize. Delegate responsibilities that drain your energy whenever possible. Focus on tasks that match your strengths and interests. Dr. Marcus Buckingham's strengths-based leadership model highlights the importance of leaders concentrating on tasks that leverage their natural talents, keeping passion strong and alive.

4. Lead with enthusiasm without being performative.
Authenticity is important. Teams can tell immediately when enthusiasm is fake. True passion comes naturally from belief and dedication, not forced cheerfulness. A leader I coached, whose enthusiasm initially seemed fake, learned that being honest about challenges, along with showing optimism about overcoming them, built real credibility and kept passion alive.

5. Celebrate mission milestones—not just metrics.
Metrics measure success, but milestones mark meaningful progress. Celebrate moments that truly resonate emotionally with the team. One executive I advised turned quarterly meetings into mission celebrations, highlighting specific stories of people whose lives were positively impacted. This fostered genuine passion by reminding everyone of their collective achievements.

TEAM APPLICATION

- Ask: "What part of our mission excites you most?"
- Tell origin stories that remind the team why it matters.
- Create passion projects alongside performance goals.

LEADERSHIP REFLECTION

Where do I need to reignite my passion—and how will I do it?

ONE-LINER TO REMEMBER

"Passion doesn't come from the position—it comes from the purpose."

CHAPTER 12
CONFIDENT - BELIEVING IN YOURSELF SO OTHERS CAN TOO

OPENING THOUGHT

Confidence isn't about having all the answers; it's about trusting yourself while staying open to growth. It's the quiet confidence that you belong in the room, even as you keep learning, asking questions, and evolving.

Throughout my career, I've worked with leaders at all levels—from experienced executives guiding large organizations to new managers taking on leadership roles for the first time—and I've observed a consistent truth: Confidence distinguishes leaders who make an impact from those who only hold titles. But it's not the kind of confidence that is loud, forceful, or driven by ego. True confidence is steady, calm, and deeply rooted in self-awareness.

It's the confidence that enables a leader to say, "I don't know, but I will find out." It's what gives a leader the courage to listen before speaking, to ask for feedback without becoming defensive, and to lead with humility while still maintaining high standards. It is the presence that reassures teams during moments of uncertainty, reminding them, "We will figure this out together."

Early in my career, I made a common mistake: I confused confidence with having all the answers and appearing flawless. I believed being a leader meant never showing doubt or vulnerability. It didn't take long to realize that this façade was unsustainable and unhelpful. It kept me from learning and created a barrier between me and the people I was trying to lead.

It was only when I started to embrace the truth that real confidence comes from admitting what I didn't know and committing to learn that my leadership began to change. I became more approachable, curious, and connected with those around me. I stopped just performing leadership and started practicing it.

This shift didn't just alter how I advised others; it changed the way I carried myself in every room I entered. I learned that people don't trust leaders who act like they know it all; they trust leaders who are honest, willing to keep learning, and courageous enough to stay steady in the face of challenges.

Confidence, in its purest form, creates space for others to grow. It demonstrates what it means to lead with strength and humility, to stand firm in your values while staying adaptable, and to pursue excellence without losing authenticity.

If you want to lead with impact, develop a confidence that builds trust, encourages growth, and empowers your team to give their best. Because leadership isn't about knowing everything; it's about showing up fully and helping others find the courage to do the same.

WHY THIS MATTERS

People won't believe in your leadership if you don't show confidence. Confidence is what allows your team to move forward with clarity and conviction, especially when everything around them is changing. In a world marked by constant disruption—from technological advances to global crises to rapidly changing markets—teams need leaders who can stay steady, not because they know everything, but because they trust their ability to figure it out.

Without confidence, leaders leave their teams adrift, unsure of what to do next and afraid to take action. With confidence, leaders become a stabilizing force, helping people navigate change with a sense of purpose and direction.

Stanford Professor Albert Bandura's groundbreaking research highlights this fact. His work on self-efficacy—our belief in our ability to do what's necessary—shows that leaders with high self-efficacy motivate, inspire resilience, and boost productivity within their teams. When leaders confidently face challenges, their teams tend to do the same, seeing obstacles as chances to learn and grow rather than threats to avoid.

Confidence isn't about having all the answers. It's about showing your team that you believe in your mission, your people, and your shared ability to overcome challenges together. It inspires trust, eases anxiety, and encourages others to step up and lead confidently as well.

People naturally pick up emotional signals from their leaders, especially during uncertain times or high-pressure moments. They observe your tone, body language, and your willingness to press forward. I have seen firsthand, in boardrooms and on the front lines, how a single leader's confident presence can change the culture of an entire organization. It's often not just the words, but the conviction behind them that motivates people to act.

When you lead with confidence, you aren't just managing the present—you are shaping the future. You are creating an environment where people feel safe enough to take risks, share ideas, and contribute their best, knowing they are anchored by a leader who believes in the mission and in them.

That is why confidence is important in leadership. It isn't about you; it's about the people you lead and the environment you create for them to succeed, even when the way forward is uncertain.

WHAT IT LOOKS LIKE

Confident leadership manifests itself in several key behaviors that distinguish effective leaders from the merely adequate:

- You communicate decisions clearly and calmly. In one organization I advised, the CEO had an exceptional ability to convey complex strategies in simple, confident terms. His clarity eased anxiety during mergers and organizational changes, allowing his team to focus on execution instead of worry.
- You don't shy away from difficult conversations. One executive I coached hesitated to address underperformance. After gaining confidence through practice and reflection, he approached tough conversations constructively instead of avoiding them. The team responded with greater respect and improved performance, showing that confidence in handling hard situations is contagious.
- You recognize your strengths without arrogance. Effective leaders confidently acknowledge their expertise, not to boast, but to empower their teams. By openly showcasing their skills, leaders set a standard for others to do the same and leverage their own strengths.
- You act without waiting for perfection. Leadership often involves navigating uncertainty. Confident leaders recognize when to act decisively with the best information available instead of stalling for perfection. This proactive approach builds momentum, allowing the team to adjust dynamically rather than stagnate.
- You lead with self-awareness, not self-doubt. Self-awareness—understanding your emotions, strengths, limitations, and values—is key to genuine confidence. Leaders who develop deep self-awareness lead without the burden of self-doubt, fostering an environment of openness and continuous growth.

WHAT HAPPENS WITHOUT IT

The absence of confidence, unfortunately, carries significant costs:

- Teams hesitate or second-guess themselves. Without a confident leader to reassure them, teams waste energy in endless deliberation and second-guessing instead of taking productive action.
- Decision-making slows or stalls. From my experience consulting for a tech startup, the CEO's lack of confidence caused decision paralysis. Projects delayed, competitors moved ahead, and morale dropped. Confidence is the remedy for stagnation.
- Fear of failure prevents taking action. A confident leader views failure as a chance to learn. Without this mindset, teams shy away from risks, hindering innovation.
- Insecurity fosters comparison instead of collaboration. Leaders who lack confidence unintentionally create competitive rather than cooperative environments. This insecurity undermines teamwork, reducing the organization's resilience.
- Talented leaders either hold back or burn out. Confidence shields against burnout by offering emotional stability and a clear purpose. Without it, talented individuals tend to withdraw or exhaust themselves in the cycle of overcompensation and insecurity.

HOW TO LEAD WITH CONFIDENCE

Building genuine confidence is a deliberate process. Here are effective strategies I've recommended to leaders:

1. Reflect on past wins—remind yourself of your progress. Regularly reviewing accomplishments strengthens belief in your abilities. A study published in the Journal of Applied Psychology confirms that reflecting positively on past successes boosts self-efficacy significantly (Stajkovic and Luthans 1998).
2. Prepare thoroughly so you can speak confidently. Preparation is a quiet yet strong foundation of confidence. Leaders who dedicate time to preparation speak with clarity and certainty, boosting their credibility and influence.
3. Say "I don't know" with clarity, not shame. A confident leader openly admits gaps in knowledge. My experiences show that leaders who confidently acknowledge uncertainty foster cultures of transparency and mutual respect, where teams feel safe to admit their own vulnerabilities.
4. Invest in personal growth—know your strength. Ongoing learning keeps confidence grounded in skill. Leaders who focus on personal growth stay adaptable, resilient, and confident as their abilities evolve.
5. Encourage others to lead by demonstrating bold and respectful actions. Confidence grows as leaders empower their teams to lead confidently. By taking respectful yet assertive action themselves, leaders foster environments that value courage and initiative.

CASE-IN-POINT

I vividly remember working with a group of young leaders in our community who were stepping into new roles with a desire to make a real difference. Many of them carried a quiet fear: "Am I ready?" "Will people listen to me?" "Do I have what it takes to lead?"

During one of our sessions, a young leader shared, "I didn't feel ready, but I showed up because I believed in the people I want to serve." That moment stayed with me. It reminded me that confidence in leadership is seldom about having all the answers; it's about showing up, fully present, with the courage to learn while leading.

These young leaders didn't seek leadership for titles or fame. They led with humility, asked thoughtful questions, and prioritized listening before taking action. They didn't pretend to know everything but cared deeply about their community and the issues that mattered. They were ready to have tough conversations, build bridges, and take action even when the results were uncertain.

I watched as their confidence grew—not as a loud declaration of "I've arrived," but as a quiet, steady presence that said, "I am here, and I am willing." They believed in the potential of those they served and in each other, and in turn, people began to believe in them.

Under their leadership, we saw projects launched that addressed real needs—mentorship programs for youth, neighborhood initiatives to reduce food insecurity, and forums that gave a voice to underrepresented communities. Their confidence became contagious, inspiring others to step forward and contribute, transforming isolated efforts into collective impact.

These young leaders reminded me once again that true confidence is rooted, genuine, and profoundly impactful. It doesn't come from pretending to be fearless; it emerges from aligning your actions with your values, showing up consistently, and leading with service at the core.

When leaders believe in themselves and in the people, they serve, and their communities reflect that belief. Confidence is not an optional trait for impactful leadership; it is a skill that can be cultivated through intentional practice, reflection, and courageous action.

Confident leadership transforms teams and communities—not because it avoids uncertainty, but because it faces uncertainty with unwavering belief in the mission and the people on the journey together.

TEAM APPLICATION

- Ask: "Where do we need to lead with more confidence — individually and collectively?"
- Coach team members through imposter moments.
- Celebrate risks taken, not just results won.

LEADERSHIP REFLECTION

Where am I hesitating — not because I can't, but because I don't believe I'm ready?

ONE-LINER TO REMEMBER

"Confidence builds courage in others — lead like you believe it."

PART FOUR
THE INFLUENCE OF PRESENCE

CHAPTER 13
APPROACHABLE — MAKING YOURSELF AVAILABLE TO YOUR TEAM

OPENING THOUGHT

Being the smartest person in the room won't help if no one feels safe enough to talk to you. I've seen brilliant leaders stumble—not because they lack vision, but because their team never felt comfortable approaching them with ideas, feedback, or even a simple question.

Approachability is leadership that welcomes — not just instructs. It's the quiet but powerful ability to signal: "I'm here, and I'm listening." And in a fast-paced workplace culture where everyone's fighting for airtime, that one signal might be the most important one you send.

WHY THIS MATTERS

Early in my consulting career, I worked with a senior leader at a midsize healthcare organization. She had it all—an Ivy League degree, decades of experience, and a strategic mind that could outthink anyone in the boardroom. Yet her team was stuck. They second-guessed decisions, avoided tough conversations, and churned at a rapid pace.

After a series of one-on-ones, the pattern became clear: they were afraid of her. Not because she yelled or belittled—because she emitted an attitude that said, "Don't waste my time." And so, they didn't. They kept concerns to themselves. They only shared her pre-screened ideas. They stayed surface-level and safe.

Psychological safety—a term created by Harvard professor Amy Edmondson—refers to an environment where people feel comfortable taking interpersonal risks. Studies have demonstrated that high-performing teams aren't just intelligent; they're psychologically safe. Edmondson discovered that in hospitals, for instance, units with higher error rates were actually safer because team members were more willing to speak up and report mistakes (Edmondson, 1999).

Approachability is the doorway to that safety.

When you are approachable:

- People bring their concerns before they become crises.
- Creative thinking increases.
- Trust becomes a cultural norm, not a lucky accident.

You stop being just the leader with authority. You become the leader with access. And when people have access to you, they align with you.

WHAT IT LOOKS LIKE

So, what does it look like to be truly approachable?

Let me break it down practically:

Open Body Language and Eye Contact
This might seem like basic communication theory, but body language has a real psychological effect. According to Dr. Albert Mehrabian's communication model, 55% of communication is non-verbal. People interpret your crossed arms, turned away, or

wandering eyes as closed off. Conversely, steady eye contact, a slight lean forward, or uncrossed arms send the silent message: "I'm here. I'm listening."

Inviting Questions, Not Just Providing Answers
I once attended a team meeting where the manager rattled off updates like a news anchor. When someone shyly raised a concern, he responded with: "Already handled. Next." The team shut down. What could've been a vital piece of insight was lost to the room. Contrast that with another leader I observed who wrapped every meeting with: "What am I missing? What are we not seeing here?" That question opened a floodgate of innovation.

Tone That Remains Fair and Calm — Even When Things Get Difficult
People aren't paying attention to your tone during easy times. They notice it when someone drops the ball, stress is high, or deadlines are missed. Being able to keep a consistent tone of fairness—even when giving tough feedback—makes you more trustworthy. One study in the Journal of Organizational Behavior found that "interactional justice," or the perception of fairness in interpersonal treatment, greatly increases employee satisfaction and commitment (Colquitt, 2001).

Availability, Not Just Visibility
It's easy to say your "door is always open," but if people never feel safe enough to knock, what's the point? True availability is intentional. It means carving out real time in your calendar for informal check-ins. It means responding to messages with curiosity, not irritation. It means showing up—not just being seen.

Making Time for the Small Stuff
There's no such thing as "just small talk" when you're building trust. Asking about someone's weekend, remembering their

child's name, or grabbing a quick coffee can create the kind of relational glue that holds teams together when things get tough. The "small stuff" is often where the big conversations begin.

WHAT HAPPENS WITHOUT IT

Let me be blunt: If you're not approachable, your leadership is running on half the fuel.

Here's what I've seen happen again and again when leaders lose approachability:

People Only Tell You What They Think You Want to Hear
And the moment that happens, you've lost. Because decisions based on filtered truth are dangerous. You start solving the wrong problems. You think you're aligned—but you're not.

Issues Go Unaddressed Until They Explode
One of my clients learned this the hard way. A minor compliance issue was noticed by a floor supervisor—but he hesitated to bring it up. "The VP doesn't want to hear about problems," he told me. That issue grew, unnoticed, until it became a full-blown operational failure. When I asked the VP why no one flagged it earlier, he shrugged: "No one told me." Exactly.

Innovation Dies Because Voices Go Unheard
Approachability fuels collaboration, and collaboration fuels innovation. Without it, you get quiet rooms, stagnant brainstorming, and missed opportunities. Google's Project Aristotle studied what made its most effective teams successful. One of the top factors? Psychological safety—the very thing that dies in an unapproachable environment (Duhigg, 2016).

You Lead in Isolation — Even When Surrounded by People
This is perhaps the most tragic consequence. You can have a team,

an office, and a calendar full of meetings—but if no one feels like they can be honest with you, you're leading alone.

HOW TO LEAD WITH APPROACHABILITY

Here are five practical steps to build approachability into your leadership style:

1. Slow Down — Make Space for Connection
Speed hinders connection. When you're always in a rush, people hesitate to interrupt—even when it matters. I often advise executives to build "white space" into their calendars. These are unscheduled 15–30-minute blocks where they can check in with people, walk the floor, or just be available.

2. Ask Open-Ended Questions Regularly
My favorite: "What's on your mind?" It's non-threatening, inviting, and allows the other person to drive the direction of the conversation. Other good ones include:
"What's something we might be missing?"
"How are you feeling about this direction?"
"If you were in my shoes, what would you do?"

3. Stay Calm and Open When People Share Hard Truths
This is a test. If someone shares something difficult and you react defensively or punishes, you teach them not to do it again. I once coached a COO who made it a habit to say, "Thank you for being honest," every time someone brought tough news. That habit alone changed the tone of his organization.

4. Be Consistent — Especially in Moments of Pressure
If you're warm and curious when things are good but become sharp and dismissive under stress, your team will learn to avoid you when it matters most. The more consistent your emotional

presence, the safer your people feel. Neuroscience research supports this: a predictable emotional environment reduces cognitive load and anxiety in team settings (Rock & Schwartz, 2006).

5. Follow Through When Someone Takes the Risk to Be Honest
Approachability without action is just performance. When someone brings something up—whether it's good, bad, or ugly—respond. Even if your answer is "I'm still working on it," your response shows them you heard them, and that's what truly matters.

CASE-IN-POINT

An executive I once worked with told me her proudest leadership moment wasn't reaching a revenue milestone or earning an industry award. It was when a junior team member—only six months into her role—knocked on her office door and said:

"I know you are busy, but I needed to talk, and I knew you would make time."

That is what approachability creates: trust in the moments that matter most. Not just when things are planned or easy—but in the unpredictable, unscripted moments where leadership gets real.

Ultimately, people do not just need your answers—they need your presence.

TEAM APPLICATION

- Ask your team anonymously: "What makes me approachable — and what does not?"
- Invite regular feedback with a no-consequence culture.
- Share stories where approachability improved an outcome.

LEADERSHIP REFLECTION

Do people bring me problems — or hide them from me?

ONE-LINER TO REMEMBER

"You can't fix what no one feels safe enough to tell you."

CHAPTER 14
RESPECT — HONORING PEOPLE FOR WHO THEY ARE

OPENING THOUGHT

Respect isn't something we give as a reward once someone "proves" themselves. It's not a currency exchanged for performance, charisma, or credentials. It's a core human attitude — choosing to see value before results.

In my years as a consultant, I've seen countless teams fail not because they lacked talent or intelligence, but because they lacked respect — the kind that values people for who they are, not just what they produce. The kind that says, "You matter here. You're not invisible."

Respect is the cornerstone of every healthy leadership relationship. Without it, authority can weaken, communication becomes superficial, and even the most well-meaning strategies may fail.

WHY THIS MATTERS

At its core, respect is recognizing someone's inherent worth. This alone changes how people show up at work. It makes teams stronger, feedback safer, and collaboration easier. When people feel respected, they don't just comply — they contribute.

I once worked at a rapidly expanding tech company where the CTO habitually called junior engineers "the kids." Initially, it seemed harmless — perhaps even playful. However, over time, those "kids" stopped sharing their best ideas during meetings. Some left the company. Others emotionally disengaged. A talented intern who had created a tool that saved the company tens of thousands of dollars later told me, "It's hard to keep offering ideas when you don't feel taken seriously."

Respect builds the bridge that every meaningful conversation must cross. Without it, people hesitate. They protect themselves. They withhold. They resist change — not because they don't care, but because they don't feel cared for.

Research supports this as well. A 2014 study in Harvard Business Review surveyed nearly 20,000 employees worldwide. The top behavior employees wanted from their leaders? Respect. It wasn't higher pay, more feedback, or better career opportunities — it was the fundamental human need to feel seen and valued (Porath, 2014).

WHAT IT LOOKS LIKE

So, what does respect look like in practice? It's simple, but purposeful.

You listen without interrupting. That might seem basic, but you'd be surprised at how many leaders are halfway through forming their next point while the other person is still talking. Listening—real listening—says, "You matter enough for me to give you my full attention."

You consider every role to be essential. And I mean every role — from the receptionist to the VP. I recall watching a senior executive who always made a point to walk the customer service floor and ask agents how their day was going. He didn't do it for show — he did it because he genuinely believed their work was mission-critical. And guess what? Those teams had the lowest turnover in the company.

You treat everyone with the same level of respect. Titles shouldn't give you a reason to treat people differently. One of the best compliments I ever received about a CEO I coached came from a cafeteria worker: "He talks to me like I'm the most important person in the building." That's not just good manners — it's good leadership.

You correct in private, not in public. Public shaming may win the moment, but it loses the person. Respect holds others accountable while preserving their dignity.

And finally, you establish boundaries — both yours and others'. Respect isn't about being a pushover. It isn't about people-pleasing or saying yes to everything. In fact, genuine respect thrives when boundaries are clear. When people see you honor your time, your energy, and your values — and when you do the same for theirs — trust builds.

WHAT HAPPENS WITHOUT IT

Lacking respect, the culture becomes harsh. People feel small, ignored, or treated as tokens. They start to wonder, "Do I really belong here?" When that question goes unanswered, they gradually fade away — sometimes physically, but more often emotionally.

Trust diminishes even when performance appears strong. I've worked with teams that hit their KPIs but were quietly burning out, disengaging, and losing faith in leadership. On paper, everything looked excellent. In reality, they were on the brink of collapse.

Marginalized voices tend to withdraw first. Those who already have to work harder to be heard — women, people of color, LGBTQ+ team members, introverts — they pick up on the room's vibe faster than anyone else. If the culture lacks respect, they will choose to step back — not because they aren't capable, but because they do not feel valued.

Conflict turns personal rather than constructive. Disagreements shift from being about ideas to being about identity. Egos grow larger. Silos develop. Office politics flourish where respect is lacking.

And worst of all, the team's culture becomes guarded—political and performative. People say what they think you want to hear, not what you need to know.

HOW TO LEAD WITH RESPECT

So, how do we course-correct? How do we lead with respect in a way that reshapes culture?

1. Don't just hear people — honor them.
This means going beyond simple transactions. It means asking how someone's weekend was and truly listening. It means remembering that your colleague cares for an aging parent, or that your employee just celebrated their five-year anniversary. Honor isn't complicated — it's just intentional.

2. Offer feedback that maintains dignity.
You can be honest without being harsh. Say what needs to be said, but do so thoughtfully. A helpful rule I follow: Never give feedback in a tone you'd dislike receiving. How we say things is just as important as what we say.

3. Avoid sarcasm, gossip, and dismissive tones.
These may seem like small things, but they quickly damage culture. Sarcasm, especially from those in authority, often causes confusion or hurts more than it amuses. Gossip fosters shadows. Dismissiveness shuts people down before they can even start. Respect means cleaning up our communication.

4. Acknowledge ideas even when you disagree.
You don't have to follow every suggestion. But recognizing some-

one's thinking — "That's an interesting angle" or "I appreciate you bringing that up" — shows you value their input. People will keep sharing ideas when they know they won't face ridicule for them.

5. Protect the team's culture — even when no one's watching.
Respect doesn't end when the room empties. It's how you speak about others when they're not present. It's refusing to laugh at demeaning jokes or let microaggressions go unnoticed. It's maintaining the standard, even — especially — in private.

CASE-IN-POINT

A leader I truly admire once said, "I knew my respect mattered when I watched how a janitor responded to the CEO — like he mattered."

That CEO didn't just send appreciation emails during Employee Recognition Week. He knew everyone's name, asked about their families, and expressed gratitude — every single day.

He didn't just "model humility." He fostered a culture of respect that went deeper than paychecks. The janitor didn't stay for the wages. He stayed because he felt like he belonged.

There's something powerful that occurs when people don't need to earn your respect — when it's given freely and consistently because they are human.

TEAM APPLICATION

- Ask the team: "What does respect look and sound like here?"
- Co-create norms around disagreement and dialogue.
- Acknowledge moments where someone modeled high respect under stress.

LEADERSHIP REFLECTION

Do people leave interactions with me feeling bigger — or smaller?

ONE-LINER TO REMEMBER

"Respect isn't something people earn from you — it's something they should never lose from you."

CHAPTER 15
CONSISTENCY — SHOWING UP WITH STEADINESS AND INTENTIONALITY

OPENING THOUGHT

Consistency builds confidence and trust.

It tells your team, "You can count on me — not just sometimes, but every time."

I've attended enough boardrooms, workshops, and coaching sessions to know this: brilliance can grab your team's attention, but consistency is what maintains their trust. It's not about being perfect — it's about being predictable in the best ways. When people know who you are and what you'll bring into the room, you create something far more valuable than hype. You build reliability. If there's one thing that can work against you as a leader, it's people not being able to count on you, especially when the going gets tough.

WHY THIS MATTERS

Let me take you back to a leadership offsite I led for a rapidly growing company. Their CEO was a firecracker—bold, visionary, the kind of leader who made people believe in moonshots. But when I interviewed his senior team beforehand, I kept hearing the same thing.

"We never know what version of him is going to show up." He is inconsistent!

That inconsistency didn't come from incompetence or lack of care. It was caused by unmanaged stress, reactive decision-making, and a failure to self-regulate. This put his team in a constant state of emotional whiplash. One week, he'd praise a new product direction; the next, he'd scrap it entirely. One quarter, he pushed for bold experimentation; the next, he punished failure.

Anxious teams avoid innovation. They stick to their own tasks and focus on self-protection.

When leaders act unpredictably — when emotions, tone, or follow-through vary greatly — people stop engaging openly. They spend more time managing your mood than advancing your mission. And here's the cost: inconsistent leadership damages psychological safety, which is the top predictor of high-performing teams, according to Google's renowned Project Aristotle study (Duhigg 2016).

Consistency isn't about robotic behavior. It's about *creating safety*. It allows people to lean into their roles, speak honestly, and trust that they're on solid ground — even when challenges come up.

WHAT IT LOOKS LIKE

Here's what I've learned about what consistency looks like in action:

1. You follow through on what you say. Your audio must match your video. If you say you'll check in by Friday, you need to check in by then. If you say the meeting will start at 9:00 a.m., you should be there by 8:58. The small things are the big things. Trust is built through the small things.

2. You lead with the same energy on tough days as you do on

good days.
No, you don't have to fake happiness. But you do need to show up fully — not retreat into emotional shutdown just because things are hard. Consistency in showing up matters more than consistency in mood.

3. You uphold standards, even when no one's watching.
Do you give feedback just when it's easy? Or even when it's awkward but necessary? I've watched cultures rot because leaders stopped enforcing the very values they printed on their walls.

4. You check your tone, not just your tasks.
Your words may say, "Great job," but if your tone is cold or dismissive, your team hears a very different message. Being emotionally steady in your tone — especially in correction — reinforces your credibility.

5. You don't "vanish" under pressure.
The true test of consistency is who you are when the heat is on. Are you accessible? Communicative? Or do you go dark, leaving your team to guess? Being available in the chaos tells people, "I'm in this with you."

WHAT HAPPENS WITHOUT IT

Let's be honest. We've all seen what happens when consistency disappears from leadership.

1. Teams lose trust.
When you don't follow through — when you say one thing and do another — people stop believing your words. And the moment trust begins to erode, alignment and productivity decline.

2. People walk on eggshells.
They start hedging in meetings. They over-prepare simple emails

just to "get the tone right." They withhold ideas, fearing they'll hit a bad mood or a moving target.

3. Morale becomes unstable.
When your energy fluctuates wildly, it becomes contagious. A moody leader creates a moody culture — people mirror what they see. Suddenly, morale isn't based on mission or momentum — it's based on your vibe that day.

4. Culture shifts based on moods, not values.
This is the silent killer. When your values are no longer the standard, and people start adapting to your emotional state instead, you've stopped leading and begun reacting. Cultures should be anchored, not adrift.

5. Small issues can grow into bigger problems.
Inconsistent responses make it difficult for people to predict how issues will be handled. As a result, they either hide problems or wait too long to bring them up — and what could have been a minor adjustment turns into a full-blown crisis.

HOW TO LEAD WITH CONSISTENCY

Now, let's shift from diagnosis to taking action. How can you become the kind of leader people trust?

1. Build and follow daily leadership rhythms
Consistency relies on structure. Establish daily and weekly routines for check-ins, feedback, and communication. This doesn't mean micromanaging; it means people understand when and how they'll hear from you. It's the difference between chaos and rhythm.
One of the most successful routines I've helped clients create is a "Leadership Dashboard" — a straightforward daily list of the top 3 leadership behaviors they aim to embody. For example:

- Did I make meaningful contact with my team today?
- Did I deliver feedback that was due?
- Did I start and end the day with intentional tone?

It sounds basic, but structure fuels steadiness.

2. Let your values drive decisions, not your emotions
Your values are your true north. They don't change with the weather. Write them down. Say them out loud. Use them to evaluate decisions. When you're tired or triggered, your emotions may demand control. That's when you remind yourself: I'm a leader, not a reactor.
Case in point — The Rotary Club has The Four-Way Test. 1. Is it the TRUTH? 2. Is it FAIR to all concerned? 3. Will it build Goodwill and Better Friendships? 4. Will it be BENEFICIAL to all concerned? A "Values Filter." When tensions run high or pressure threatens to compromise standards, return to your filter: Does this person align with our cultural values of collaboration, humility, and learning? It will save you from some very costly decisions.

3. Be predictable in the right ways
People don't want a monotone robot. But they do want emotional predictability. Calm. Fairness. Clarity. You can still surprise your team with creativity — just don't surprise them with volatility. Predictability in behavior doesn't make you boring; It makes you *trusted*.

4. Document expectations and model them
When you define what "good" looks like, it removes uncertainty. Your team shouldn't have to guess your intentions. If you want people to communicate openly, you need to lead with transparent updates. If collaboration is important, avoid isolating yourself during decision-making.
Document. Communicate. Model. Repeat.

5. Self-regulate before you interact

Leadership begins before you step into the room. It starts with the 10 seconds you take to breathe deeply, ground yourself, and remind yourself of who you want to be. Emotional regulation isn't weakness — it's leadership at its highest level.

Neuroscientist Dr. Lisa Feldman Barrett reminds us that emotions aren't just reactions — they are shaped by the stories we tell ourselves (Barrett 2017). You can change your state by shifting your perspective. Before entering a difficult meeting, take a moment to ask yourself:

- What's the story I'm telling myself?
- Is that the most helpful story right now?
- What do *they* need from me in this moment?

You'll show up differently — and more consistently.

CASE-IN-POINT

One of the most impactful things I've ever heard in a workplace was from a young team member describing her manager:

"He doesn't change with the wind. I always know I can trust how he'll respond — even when I mess up."

That statement stuck with me because it wasn't about charisma or even technical skill. It was about *presence*.

Because that manager didn't panic under pressure or shame people for mistakes, his team brought him issues early. They told the truth, even when it was hard. They experimented more — and grew faster.

It wasn't perfection that made him great. It was *consistency*.

That's the kind of leader I aim to be.

And it's the kind of leader our teams need today — in a world that's already unpredictable enough.

TEAM APPLICATION

- Ask your team: "What's one thing I do consistently that helps you — and one I should improve?"
- Define what consistency looks like in your team's habits and meetings.
- Highlight and reward consistent behaviors in peers, not just standout moments.

LEADERSHIP REFLECTION

Is my team guessing who I'll be today — or do they know what I stand for?

ONE-LINER TO REMEMBER

"Consistency is what makes your values believable."

CHAPTER 16
PRESENCE – BE WHERE YOUR FEET ARE

OPENING THOUGHT

Your presence is your power, not your position or title, but your full, focused presence in the moments that matter most.

I've coached Fortune 500 executives, scrappy startup founders, government leaders, and nonprofit directors—and there's one thing they all have in common. The people they lead are constantly watching and feeling for *presence*. Not prestige. Not performance metrics. But presence.

Being fully present with people is another underrated leadership skill in today's world. We live in a distraction-filled environment, where screens constantly buzz, the next meeting is always looming, and busyness is often mistaken for value. But if you want to build trust, deepen influence, and motivate people—not just count numbers—presence is where it begins.

WHY THIS MATTERS

I'll be honest: people notice when you're not really paying attention. They might not say anything, but they can tell. It shows in your glazed eyes, how your phone lights up and distracts you during conversations, or your habit of interrupting or rushing through talks. And even when you're there physically, they sense your absence—because they remember it.

Presence says:

"You matter. Right now. More than anything else in this moment."

Leadership isn't just about vision, strategy, or authority. It's about the ability to make people feel truly seen. When leaders are fully present, they naturally build trust. They create clarity by understanding the real issues. They foster connection because the people around them feel they're not just being managed—they're being genuinely met.

Psychologist Carl Rogers, in his groundbreaking work on person-centered therapy, emphasized the concept of "unconditional positive regard"—the ability to fully listen and be present without judgment. He wrote that presence "is the most precious gift we can offer each other" (Rogers, 1961). The same holds true in leadership. Your presence *is* your gift.

WHAT IT LOOKS LIKE

Here's what I've seen strong, present leaders consistently do:

You put your phone down and make eye contact
It sounds simple, but in our notification-filled world, this is revolutionary. It says, "I'm not checking out—I'm tuning in."

You listen patiently without rushing
You don't interrupt to finish people's sentences or jump in to solve the problem. You allow them to express their thoughts fully. You offer your time as proof of their value.

You arrive early — not just on time
Not to earn points, but because showing up requires preparation.

You can't rush from one meeting to another and expect to stay grounded.

You participate in meetings as if they are important
Not just nodding and multitasking, but asking questions, sharing ideas, and showing attentiveness.

You're not multitasking while someone is sharing
A 2009 Stanford study found that people who multitask perform worse on tasks requiring memory and attention than those who don't (Ophir, Nass, & Wagner, 2009). Being present is not just polite — it's productive.

WHAT HAPPENS WITHOUT IT

When presence is absent, the ripple effects are real:

People feel dismissed or unimportant
They begin second-guessing themselves, or even worse, they stop showing up as their full selves. Miscommunication increases because you weren't truly listening, and they noticed. Now, you're making decisions based on assumptions.

You overlook signs of burnout, conflict, or brilliance
The employee quietly struggling? You didn't notice. The team member with a million-dollar idea? You rushed them. The rising tension between departments? You tuned it out. Your team feels like they're managing upward — not being led, because they're carrying the emotional labor of getting your attention.

Trust erodes
And once it begins to break down, no spreadsheet or strategic plan can keep your team united. Presence is the foundation of psychological safety—a term coined by Harvard Business School

professor Amy Edmondson, who found that teams with high psychological safety are more innovative and productive because members feel safe to take risks (Edmondson, 1999). Presence creates that safety.

HOW TO LEAD WITH PRESENCE

So how do you accomplish this in the chaos of modern leadership?

1. Block quiet time before high-stakes conversations
You can't go from a fire drill to a heart-to-heart without catching your breath. Even five minutes of silence before a big meeting can help you reset and show up more grounded. I've made this a non-negotiable before every board meeting, difficult employee conversation, or client pitch.

2. Treat small conversations like big moments
I once had a CEO tell me he had a "drive-by" chat with a junior employee that changed his entire perspective on a project. "She felt heard," he said, "and I got a front-row seat into the customer experience." Big moments are often hidden in small interactions.

3. Limit distractions — phone, notifications, interruptions
Put your phone face down—or better yet, out of sight. Silence notifications. Close your laptop if you're not presenting. Presence is a discipline of elimination.

4. Schedule margin in your day so you're not always rushing
Back-to-back meetings aren't something to be proud of. They lead to mental fog. You need breaks between meetings to process, refocus, and be present for the next person instead of carrying over the last meeting's stress.

5. Train yourself to focus on people — not just tasks

Yes, deliverables matter. But people drive deliverables. When you see your team as humans first—not just resources—you lead with empathy. And empathy improves results. One study by DDI, a global leadership firm, found that empathy is the most critical factor in overall performance among leaders (DDI, 2016).

CASE-IN-POINT

One of the most powerful leadership turnarounds I've ever witnessed came from a senior VP at a tech firm. Let's call him Aaron. Brilliant strategist. Respected in the C-suite. But his team was suffering.

One afternoon, during a culture feedback session I facilitated, a brave mid-level manager said, "Aaron, you're in the room, but we can tell you're not with us." You could hear a pin drop.

To his credit, Aaron didn't get defensive. He asked for examples. They told him: He checked his phone in meetings. He seemed rushed. He was hard to schedule one-on-ones with. He didn't remember details of their conversations. "We don't need more emails from you," someone said. "We need *you*."

That moment became a turning point.

Aaron started blocking off "presence hours" in his calendar—uninterrupted time just to walk the floor, check in with people, and *listen*. He shortened his meetings so he could show up more intentionally. He asked his EA to gatekeep distractions. And over the next six months, you could feel the change.

Retention went up. Engagement scores jumped. Two high-potential leaders who were thinking about quitting decided to stay—and later got promoted. "It wasn't a strategy shift," one told me. "It was a presence shift."

TEAM APPLICATION

- Ask your team: "What does presence look like to you?"
- Host "no-device" meetings to promote attention.

- Set leadership norms for presence during conflict, coaching, and check-ins.

LEADERSHIP REFLECTION

Am I giving people my presence — or just my time?

ONE-LINER TO REMEMBER

> "Presence is the way your people measure whether they matter to you."

PART FIVE
THE LEGACY OF LEADERSHIP

CHAPTER 17
EMPOWERMENT — DEVELOPING LEADERS, NOT JUST FOLLOWERS

I'VE SPENT my entire career observing the difference between leaders who keep the spotlight on themselves and those who give out flashlights so others can shine. The first type builds followers, while the second creates leaders—and that's the only kind of leadership that endures.

Empowerment is not about relinquishing all control. It's about offering enough trust, responsibility, and authority so that others can develop into their full potential. And here's the truth: if you're the only one in the room who can decide, solve a problem, or move the mission forward, you're not leading—you're bottlenecking.

WHY EMPOWERMENT MATTERS

When you empower others, you expand leadership. Instead of one leader with ten supporters, you have ten leaders who can advance the mission—either together or individually.

In every organization I've worked with, the most sustainable success came from leaders who understood that their job wasn't to be the hero, but to build heroes.

Empowerment is a trust exercise. You're telling someone, "I believe in your judgment, I trust your abilities, and I'm willing to let you learn through action — not just observation."

Gallup's research shows that employees who strongly agree they have the freedom to make decisions are 43% more engaged and 37% more likely to stay for over three years. The key word there is "freedom." But freedom without support is just abandonment. Empowerment works when it's paired with coaching, accountability, and a clear sense of purpose.

CASE-IN-POINT: THE CONFERENCE THAT CHANGED A CAREER

A few years back, I was leading a high-profile project for a client. The final presentation was the kind that could open new doors—or shut them—for both of us. My instinct was to take the stage myself. I knew the content, the stakes, and the client well. But I also realized this was a great chance to help someone else grow.

I called in one of my team members, a talented young leader named Maria. She had the skills, but lacked confidence. I told her, "You're delivering the keynote. I'll be here to support you, but the stage is yours."

She froze. "What if I mess it up?"

I smiled and said, "Then we'll fix it together. But you're ready."

We spent weeks preparing—role-playing questions, refining slides, and even practicing how to stand and breathe when nerves hit. When the day arrived, Maria stood in front of 300 executives and delivered a message so powerful that two companies approached her afterward for consulting work.

Here's the thing—those offers weren't for me. They were for her. And that's exactly how it should be. She grew, our client grew, and because she was empowered, she became an ambassador for the mission long after the event ended.

A PERSONAL LESSON IN LETTING GO

Early in my military career, I had a squad leader who never let anyone else run drills. He was good—sharp, disciplined, and competent. But the day he got sick, the entire unit stumbled. No one else knew the cadence, and no one had practiced making the calls under pressure.

When I eventually took on a leadership role, I remembered that. I made it my goal to ensure that no one— not even myself— was the single point of failure. Every member of my unit had to know how to lead a drill, run a briefing, or make a field decision. I wasn't just training them to follow orders—I was training them to give them.

That mindset carried over into my civilian leadership role. I want my team to be so well-prepared that if I disappear for a month, the mission doesn't just survive — it thrives.

WHAT EMPOWERMENT IS (AND ISN'T)

- **It is**: Trust plus responsibility plus support.
- **It isn't**: "Sink or swim" leadership where you throw someone into the deep end without a life jacket.
- **It is**: Sharing decision-making power and giving others room to own their results.
- **It isn't**: Abdicating your role as a leader or dodging accountability.

WHAT IT LOOKS LIKE IN ACTION

1. **Delegating with clarity** – Don't just hand over a task; hand over the "why" behind it. People commit more when they understand the purpose.
2. **Providing resources, not just responsibility** – Training,

information, access, and time are the fuel for empowerment.
3. **Giving real authority** – If you delegate a project but retain all approval power, you haven't empowered—you've assigned.
4. **Backing their decisions publicly** – If they make the call, stand beside them in front of others. Correct privately, support publicly.
5. **Encouraging decision-making before perfection** – Let people act without waiting for flawless conditions.

THE RISK AND THE REWARD

I've heard leaders say, "I'd love to empower my team, but what if they fail?" My response is always the same: They will. So will you. Failure is part of leadership. The real question is, "Will you give them a safe place to fail forward?"

One of my clients, a regional operations director, was known for controlling every decision. She was intelligent, quick, and capable—but her team was disengaged, and turnover was high. We tried a new method: each month, one team member would take full ownership of a project, including presenting results to leadership.

The first month was tough. Deadlines were missed, and details fell through the cracks. But instead of taking control away from the team, she guided them through the recovery process. By month three, they were meeting deadlines early and presenting confidently. Her turnover decreased by 40% in a year—not because salaries increased, but because employees felt trusted.

THREE QUESTIONS EVERY EMPOWERING LEADER ASKS

1. *Who can I trust with this decision?*
2. *What resources do they need to succeed?*
3. *How will I support them without taking over?*

PRACTICAL WAYS TO EMPOWER STARTING TODAY

- Ask a team member to lead the next meeting.
- Delegate a client presentation to a junior colleague with your full prep support.
- Let your team set the agenda for your one-on-one.
- Say "You decide" more often—and mean it.
- Share your own decision-making process so others learn how to think, not just what to do.

EMPOWERMENT IN ACTION: A LEADERSHIP CHALLENGE

If empowerment is to be more than just a buzzword, you must start practicing it right away. Here's a challenge I give to executives, new managers, and community leaders alike — it works in every setting.

Step 1 – Identify a Growth Opportunity for Someone Else
Think about your team right now. Who has the potential to take on more but hasn't had the chance? Write their name down.

Step 2 – Choose a Genuine Responsibility
Not just busy work. Not a "practice project" no one cares about. Pick something visible and meaningful—something that truly supports the mission.

Step 3 – Equip, Don't Abandon
Give them the *why*, the resources, and the authority to make decisions. Ask, "What do you need from me to succeed?" and actually deliver on it.

Step 4 – Let Them Lead
Resist the urge to intervene unless it's truly needed. Allow them to take ownership. Offer support privately, stand with them publicly.

Step 5 – Debrief as a Team

After the project or task concludes, gather to discuss:

- What worked well?
- What challenges came up?
- What would they do differently next time?

LEADER'S REFLECTION

Answer these in your journal:

1. When was the last time I gave someone else authority over something important?
2. What's holding me back from empowering more often —fear, perfectionism, time, or trust?
3. How would my team's capacity change if I empowered them more consistently?

TEAM APPLICATION

At your next team meeting, share one decision or responsibility you're intentionally handing over—and why. Ask each team member to do the same within the next month.

ONE-LINER TO REMEMBER

"Empowerment isn't giving people work—it's giving them ownership."

FINAL THOUGHT

Empowerment isn't about letting go of control—it's about letting go of ego. It's the difference between a leader who says, *"Look at what I've done"* and a leader who says, *"Look at what they've become."*

If you want your leadership to outlast you, you have to build other leaders. That starts with giving people more than tasks. It starts with giving them trust, ownership, and the chance to rise.

CHAPTER 18
GROWTH MINDSET – CHOOSING LEARNING OVER LIMITATION

I'VE WORKED with CEOs who built billion-dollar companies and managers leading ten-person teams. Some had identical technical skills, resources, and market conditions—but their results couldn't have been more different.

The difference?
A growth mindset.

A growth mindset is the belief that your abilities can be developed through dedication, learning, and resilience—not fixed by talent alone. Leaders with a growth mindset see setbacks as lessons, feedback as fuel, and challenges as opportunities. Leaders without it? They see problems as stop signs and feedback as personal attacks.

WHY GROWTH MINDSET MATTERS FOR LEADERS

As leaders, our mindset is contagious. If you see problems as solvable, your team will too. If you treat mistakes as learning opportunities, your people will take calculated risks and innovate. But if you see every setback as a failure to be punished, you'll create a culture where people hide problems instead of fixing them.

Stanford psychologist Carol Dweck's research indicates that people with a growth mindset achieve more because they dedicate extra time and effort to overcoming challenges. In leadership, this results in better adaptability, higher employee engagement, and more enduring long-term outcomes.

I've seen it firsthand: organizations led by growth-mindset leaders recover more quickly from crises, excel in innovation, and develop more leaders internally—because their people are not afraid to try, fail, and try again.

CASE-IN-POINT: THE SALES TEAM THAT COULDN'T CLOSE

A few years ago, I worked with a mid-sized company whose sales team consistently missed targets. Morale was low, turnover was high, and management was prepared to replace half the team.

Instead of firing employees and starting over, we tried something different: a growth-mindset intervention. We held a retreat where the first rule was, "We are not here to blame—we are here to learn."

We analyzed lost deals without judgment. We practiced role-playing client objections. We invited top salespeople from other industries to share their process. Most importantly, we rephrased every missed sale as "tuition"—the cost of learning how to improve.

Three months later, close rates increased by 22%, not due to market changes, but because of a shift in mindset. The same people, same tools—just a new perspective.

A PERSONAL LESSON IN GROWTH

Early in my career, I thought my value depended on having all the answers. That worked well—until I faced a challenge I couldn't solve on my own. I remember sitting in my office late at night, frustrated because I didn't have a solution.

That's when a mentor told me something that changed my approach: "Ron, your job is not to know everything. Your job is to learn fast and lead through the learning."

From that moment, I stopped pretending I had everything figured out. I started asking better questions, seeking feedback from my team, and admitting when I needed help. Not only did my performance improve, but my team trusted me more — because they saw me modeling the very thing I was asking of them: growth over ego.

WHAT GROWTH MINDSET IS (AND ISN'T)

- **It is**: Believing skills can be learned and improved.
- **It isn't**: Believing "anything is possible" without effort.
- **It is**: Treating challenges as training, not punishment.
- **It isn't**: Avoiding accountability in the name of "learning."

WHAT IT LOOKS LIKE IN ACTION

1. Reframing mistakes as lessons – After a failed initiative, ask, "What did we learn that makes us stronger for next time?"
2. Inviting feedback regularly – Not just during performance reviews, but as a weekly rhythm.
3. Celebrating progress, not just perfection – Acknowledge when someone improves, even if they're not "there" yet.
4. Investing in development – Training, mentorship, and stretch assignments aren't luxuries—they're necessities.
5. Asking "What's next?" instead of "Who's to blame?"

CASE-IN-POINT: THE ENGINEER WHO ASKED "WHY?"

One of my clients had a young engineer who was always asking "why" in meetings. At first, leadership thought it was slowing things down. But instead of stopping him, the director encouraged it and said, "Keep asking—but be ready to help us find answers."

That change transformed the engineer into an innovator. Within two years, he had developed a process improvement that saved the company more than $2 million each year.

If they had called him a troublemaker instead of a learner, they would have lost one of their most valuable problem-solvers.

THREE LEADERSHIP PRACTICES TO BUILD A GROWTH MINDSET CULTURE

1. Model it visibly – Share what you're learning. Admit when you're wrong. Show your team you're improving, too.
2. Reward effort and improvement – Recognize persistence and creative problem-solving, not just final outcomes.
3. Normalize learning from loss – Publicly discuss lessons from setbacks so your team sees failure as data, not disgrace.

EMPOWERMENT + GROWTH MINDSET = LEADERSHIP MULTIPLIER

When empowerment (Chapter 17) combines with a growth mindset, you get an unstoppable force. Empowerment gives people the freedom to act, while a growth mindset gives them the courage to try, fail, and keep going.

I've seen teams outperform bigger, better-funded competitors because they weren't afraid to push beyond their comfort zones.

GROWTH MINDSET IN ACTION: A LEADERSHIP CHALLENGE

Step 1 – Identify a challenge you've been avoiding. Write down one problem, decision, or initiative you've been delaying because you don't feel "ready."

Step 2 – Ask three learning questions

- What's one thing I can try now?
- Who can I learn from?
- What will I measure to track progress?

Step 3 – Take a small, imperfect action within 48 hours
Don't wait for perfect conditions. Start with what you know and adjust as you learn.

LEADER'S REFLECTION

1. What's one skill I've been telling myself I "just don't have"?
2. How would I approach it differently if I believed I could learn it?
3. Where in my leadership have I been protecting my image instead of pursuing growth?

TEAM APPLICATION

At your next meeting, ask each person to share:

- One thing they've learned in the past month.
- How they plan to apply it in the next month.

ONE-LINER TO REMEMBER

"Your potential isn't fixed—it's fueled by how fast you're willing to learn."

CHAPTER 19
RESILIENCE — LEADING THROUGH SETBACKS WITH STRENGTH AND STEADINESS

I'VE SEEN leaders succeed when everything goes their way. The budget is healthy. The team is happy. The metrics are green. It's easy to look strong when the wind is at your back.

However, authentic leadership shows up when the wind shifts —when the numbers dip, the team fractures, or the unexpected turns your plan upside down.

Resilience isn't about avoiding storms. It's about leading through them—and emerging stronger on the other side.

WHY RESILIENCE MATTERS FOR LEADERS

When a leader lacks resilience, their team immediately feels it. Stress flows down. Doubt spreads. Panic grows. But when a leader remains steady amid uncertainty, they provide their people with something invaluable: stability.

Harvard Business Review reports that resilient leaders have teams that are 31% more engaged, 51% more adaptive, and 43% more committed to the mission—because they trust that when things get tough, their leader won't give up.

Resilience isn't a personality trait you either have or don't. It's a skill—a leadership muscle that can be built through intentional practice. Every challenge, when handled properly, makes you stronger for the next one.

CASE-IN-POINT: THE PROJECT THAT WENT SIDEWAYS

A few years ago, I was working with a client on a major system overhaul—one that affected nearly every department. We'd spent months planning. The go-live date was set. The communications plan was solid. We were ready.

Then, two weeks before the launch, our primary vendor experienced a major technical failure. The timeline exploded. Stakeholders were furious. The pressure became overwhelming.

I could have reacted like some leaders do—point fingers, assign blame, and go into damage control. Instead, I called an emergency all-hands meeting and told the team: "This is not the end of the project. This is just a plot twist. We're going to regroup, reset, and still deliver. It might not be on the original schedule, but it will be right."

We divided the work into two phases, added daily check-ins, and hired a temporary technical consultant to fill in gaps. The new timeline was tight but achievable. The team felt the difference—less panic, more focus on solving problems.

Three months later, we launched successfully. It wasn't perfect, but it was solid. And more importantly, the team had learned how to work together under pressure.

RESILIENCE I HAD TO EARN

When I moved from the military to the business world, I believed my discipline and experience would make every transition easy. I was mistaken.

I remember an early consulting engagement where I underestimated the complexity of the client's culture. I went in with a plan

I was confident would succeed—and within two weeks, it was clear it wouldn't.

I had a choice: protect my ego and push forward anyway, or admit I needed to pivot. I chose the pivot. I told the client, "We're going to reset this. Here's what I missed, and here's how I propose we adjust."

That moment was humbling, but it taught me that resilience isn't about never falling—it's about getting back up more quickly and wisely, without letting pride hold you back.

THE LAYERED NATURE OF RESILIENCE

Resilience in leadership has layers:

1. Personal Resilience – How you handle setbacks in your own life. If you can't manage personal adversity, it will show up in your professional leadership.
2. Team Resilience – How your group responds together when things go wrong. Do they freeze, fracture, or rally?
3. Organizational Resilience – The systems, culture, and mindset that allow a company to adapt to change without losing its identity or momentum.

Great leaders work on all three simultaneously.

WHAT RESILIENCE IS (AND IS NOT)

- It is: The ability to recover quickly from setbacks.
- It is not: Pretending nothing's wrong or ignoring problems.
- It is: Adjusting your approach without losing your focus.
- It is not: Sticking to a failing plan just to prove a point.

WHAT IT LOOKS LIKE IN ACTION

1. Staying calm in crisis – Your tone sets the emotional temperature of the room.
2. Pivoting without panic – Change direction decisively, but not reactively.
3. Communicating consistently – In hard times, silence breeds rumors.
4. Owning the challenge – Take responsibility for moving forward, even if the setback was not your fault.
5. Keeping perspective – Remind your team of the bigger picture and the mission beyond the moment.

CASE-IN-POINT: THE HOSPITAL TEAM THAT WOULD NOT BREAK

One of my healthcare clients faced a year of relentless challenges—staff shortages, new regulations, budget cuts. Morale was barely hanging on.

Instead of pushing harder and exhausting everyone, the hospital director took a counterintuitive step: she scheduled weekly resilience huddles. During these 15-minute stand-ups, staff could share small wins, express frustrations, and exchange solutions.

She also rotated "day-off coverage," making sure no one went more than six weeks without a full mental reset. Within nine months, patient satisfaction improved, staff turnover slowed, and the team's internal trust score jumped 24 points.

The director did not remove the challenges—she led her team through them.

HOW LEADERS CAN BUILD RESILIENCE OVER TIME

Resilience does not come from motivational posters—it comes from habits.

- Debrief challenges quickly – Do not dwell for weeks before regrouping.
- Maintain a future focus – Learn from the past but lead toward the future.
- Build your support network – Other leaders, mentors, and peers help you carry the weight.
- Practice stress management – Exercise, reflection, and rest are not extras; they are essentials.

RESILIENCE IN ACTION: A LEADERSHIP CHALLENGE

Step 1 – Identify a current stress point
Write down one thing right now that is draining your energy or testing your patience.

Step 2 – Break it down
List what you can control, what you can influence, and what you must accept.

Step 3 – Choose the next step
Commit to one action—today—that will move you forward, even slightly.

LEADER'S REFLECTION

1. How do I typically respond when things go wrong?
2. Who's watching me for cues during difficult times—and what am I showing them?
3. When was the last time I modeled calm under pressure?

TEAM APPLICATION

In your next meeting, ask your team to share one example of a time they overcame a challenge together—and what they learned from it. Capture the common themes and post them as "Our Resilience Playbook."

ONE-LINER TO REMEMBER

"Resilience is not about avoiding the storm—it is about becoming the kind of leader people trust to steer through it."

CHAPTER 20
LEGACY — LEADING BEYOND YOUR TIME

I'VE BEEN ASKED many times: "What do you want people to remember about you when you're gone?"

It is a question that stops you in your tracks. Not because it is morbid—but because it is clarifying.

Legacy is the echo of your leadership. It is not just the titles you've held, the awards on your wall, or the revenue you've generated. Legacy is how you made people feel, the opportunities you created for others, and the impact you had that continues long after you've left the room—or the role.

WHY LEGACY MATTERS IN LEADERSHIP

Titles change. Markets shift. Your "current" project will someday be someone else's "past initiative." But your influence—how you shape people, teams, and culture—can last for decades.

I've met leaders who left companies five, ten, or even twenty years ago, and yet their names still come up with respect. Not because they were perfect, but because they were intentional about what they left behind.

If you're not intentionally considering your leadership legacy, you're leaving it to luck—and luck seldom creates something worth recalling.

CASE-IN-POINT: THE LEADERSHIP RIPPLE

Years ago, I was coaching a department head at a manufacturing company. She was capable, straightforward, and deeply dedicated to her team. When she retired, her successor told me, "I walked into a culture I didn't have to rebuild, because she left me a foundation of trust and empowerment."

Here's the powerful part:

Two years later, one of *her* managers promoted a frontline supervisor, who said in his acceptance speech, "I'm here because she believed in me."

That's the ripple effect. Your legacy isn't just about who you directly influence — it's about who they continue to influence.

LEGACY I DIDN'T SEE COMING

When I was in the military, I didn't pay much attention to "legacy." I was focused on the mission right in front of me.

Years later, I ran into a soldier I had mentored early in my career. He told me, "You probably don't remember this, but during a deployment, you pulled me aside and told me I had leadership potential. That conversation changed the way I saw myself. I started taking on more responsibility, and now I'm leading my own unit."

I didn't remember the exact conversation, but he had carried it for over a decade. That's when it hit me: legacy is built in moments you might not even notice at the time.

WHAT LEGACY IS (AND ISN'T)

- It is: The lasting impact of your leadership decisions, relationships, and influence.

- It isn't: A self-written highlight reel of your career achievements.
- It is: What people *continue* to do, believe, and feel because of your leadership.
- It isn't: What people say in a farewell speech to be polite.

WHAT IT LOOKS LIKE IN ACTION

1. Developing people beyond the role they're in now – Invest in skills that will serve them long after they've left your team.
2. Building systems that outlast you – Don't just create quick fixes; create sustainable processes.
3. Modeling values you want to see replicated – People don't just remember what you said; they remember how you lived your values under pressure.
4. Documenting wisdom and lessons learned – Share knowledge so others can build on it instead of starting from scratch.

CASE-IN-POINT: THE SCHOOL SUPERINTENDENT'S GIFT

I worked with a school district where the superintendent was retiring after thirty years. On her last day, she didn't give a speech about her accomplishments. Instead, she handed every principal in the district a binder labeled "Lessons Learned the Hard Way." Inside were stories, strategies, and guiding principles she wished someone had given her.

Her message was clear: I want you to begin where I left off. That binder became the district's unofficial leadership handbook —and her influence kept shaping decisions long after she departed.

BUILDING YOUR LEGACY ON PURPOSE

Legacy doesn't happen automatically—it's the result of daily leadership choices. You build it when you:

- Decide to mentor someone instead of competing with them.
- Choose to give credit instead of take it.
- Leave tools and systems behind instead of taking them with you.
- Tell the truth, even when it's costly.
- Invest in relationships you might never personally benefit from.

THE DANGER OF AN ACCIDENTAL LEGACY

Here's the truth—everyone leaves a legacy, whether they realize it or not.

If you're not deliberate, you might leave a legacy of fear, mistrust, or missed opportunities. I've worked with organizations still dealing with the aftermath of leaders who put their own comfort above their people's growth.

The question is: Will your legacy be something people want to carry forward—or something they need to recover from?

THREE QUESTIONS FOR DEFINING YOUR LEADERSHIP LEGACY

1. If I left my role tomorrow, what would my team keep doing the same way because of me?
2. What would they immediately change?
3. Who will be leading because I led?

LEGACY IN ACTION: A LEADERSHIP CHALLENGE

Step 1 – Identify your impact goal
Write down one thing you want to be remembered for as a leader.

Step 2 – Align your daily actions
Ask yourself each week: "Did my actions this week reflect the legacy I want to leave?"

Step 3 – Pass something forward now
Don't wait until you leave a role to transfer wisdom, resources, or opportunities. Choose one thing this month to pass on to someone else.

LEADER'S REFLECTION

1. Whose leadership am I still benefiting from years later?
2. What did they do that made their influence last?
3. How can I be that kind of leader for someone else?

TEAM APPLICATION

Ask your team to identify one positive practice or principle they want to pass down to future leaders in your organization. Create a "Legacy List" and review it quarterly.

ONE-LINER TO REMEMBER

"Your leadership legacy isn't what you leave *for* people—it's what you leave *in* them."

CONCLUSION: THE IMPACT YOU LEAVE BEHIND

Leadership isn't a title you inherit or a chair you sit in—it's a presence you carry. It's the unseen weight of your influence, evaluated not by authority but by impact. Every word you speak, every silence you choose, and every decision you make quietly shapes the story people will one day tell about your leadership.

And here's the truth: that story starts long before you even realize you're writing it. Long before you're given a role or recognized with a title, your influence has already begun shaping those around you.

The last four chapters—Empowerment, Growth Mindset, Resilience, and Legacy—are not just leadership buzzwords. They are the core principles that support lasting leadership, the kind of leadership people remember not only for what it accomplished but also for how it made them feel to be led.

Empowerment is more than just delegating tasks. It's about giving people ownership—trusting them enough to help them grow beyond their current limits, and sometimes beyond what they even believe is possible. Empowerment whispers, "I believe in you," and that belief can have the power to transform lives.

Growth Mindset involves demonstrating curiosity, humility, and courage. It is the consistent belief that there's always more to learn, even if it means failing publicly and daring to try again. When leaders show they are learners too, they encourage others to take risks, stumble, and rise.

Resilience is the steady hand in the storm. It is the calm voice that says, *"We will get through this,"* when others only see chaos. Resilience teaches that setbacks don't define us—our response does. And in that response, leaders prove their strength.

Legacy is not an accident. It is intentional. It is deciding, day by day, what you will leave behind in the hearts, minds, and actions of others. Legacy is not carved in monuments or written in reports —it's carried in people.

These aren't just one-time acts; they are daily choices. Leadership shows in how you handle a missed deadline, how you greet your team in the morning, and how you share credit when things go right and take responsibility when they go wrong.

And make no mistake: someone is watching you right now. They are deciding, whether consciously or not, what kind of leader they will become—based on the example you set. You may never know their name. You may never hear how your influence shaped them. But it will.

You can't control the length of your leadership journey. Circumstances will change. Roles will evolve. Seasons will end. But you do have control over its depth, integrity, and impact.

So lead as if it truly matters—because it does.

> *Empower boldly.*
> *Learn relentlessly.*
> *Stand steady in the storm.*

And leave behind something worth carrying forward.

Because one day, years from now, someone will be asked, *"Who had the most significant impact on your life?"*

Moreover, in that quiet moment of reflection, they just might say your name.

CHAPTER 1
CITATIONS

CHAPTER One

1. Bryant, Adam. "Alan Mulally of Ford, on Teamwork and Leadership." *The New York Times*, December 8, 2010. https://www.nytimes.com/2010/12/05/business/05corner.html.

2. Covey, Stephen M. R. *The Speed of Trust: The One Thing That Changes Everything.* New York: Free Press, 2006.

3. Dirks, Kurt T., and Donald L. Ferrin. "The Role of Trust in Organizational Settings." *Organization Science* 12, no. 4 (2001): 450–467. https://doi.org/10.1287/orsc.12.4.450.10640.

4. Edmondson, Amy C. *The Fearless Organization: Creating Psychological Safety in the Workplace for Learning, Innovation, and Growth.* Hoboken, NJ: Wiley, 2019.

5. Gallup. *State of the Global Workplace: 2023 Report.* Washington, DC: Gallup, 2023. https://www.gallup.com/workplace/349484/state-of-the-global-workplace.aspx.

6. Kouzes, James M., and Barry Z. Posner. *The Leadership Challenge: How to Make Extraordinary Things Happen in Organizations.* 6th ed. Hoboken, NJ: Jossey-Bass, 2017.

7. Lencioni, Patrick. *The Five Dysfunctions of a Team: A Leadership Fable.* San Francisco: Jossey-Bass, 2002.

8. Taylor, Alex. *Driving Change: The Remarkable Resurgence of Ford Motor Company.* New York: Crown Business, 2010.

Chapter Two

1. Gallup. *State of the Global Workplace: 2023 Report.* Washington, D.C.: Gallup, 2023.

2. Worline, Monica C., and Jane E. Dutton. "How Compassionate Leaders Perform Better." *Harvard Business Review*, May 2021.

3. Gentry, William A., Regina H. Eckert, Sarah A. Stawiski, and Todd J. Weber. *The Role of Listening in Leadership.* Greensboro, NC: Center for Creative Leadership, 2016.

4. Johnson, Stefanie K., and Daniel R. Ilgen. "Leader Presence and the Impact of Attention on Employee Trust." *Journal of Applied Psychology* 101, no. 8 (2016): 1131–1145.

Chapter Three

1. Amabile, Teresa, and Steven J. Kramer. *The Progress Principle: Using Small Wins to Ignite Joy, Engagement, and Creativity at Work.* Boston: Harvard Business Review Press, 2011.

2. Barsade, Sigal G., and Olivia A. O'Neill. "Employees Who Feel Love Perform Better." *Harvard Business Review*, January 2014. https://hbr.org/2014/01/employees-who-feel-love-perform-better

3. Collins, Jim. *Good to Great: Why Some Companies Make the Leap... and Others Don't.* New York: HarperBusiness, 2001.

4. Deloitte Insights. *2020 Global Human Capital Trends: The Social Enterprise at Work: Paradox as a Path Forward.* Deloitte Development LLC, 2020. https://www2.deloitte.com/us/en/insights/focus/human-capital-trends/2020.html

5. Dweck, Carol S. *Mindset: The New Psychology of Success.* New York: Random House, 2006.

6. Edmondson, Amy C. "Psychological Safety and Learning Behavior in Work Teams." *Administrative Science Quarterly* 44, no. 2 (1999): 350–383. https://doi.org/10.2307/2666999

7. Gallup. *State of the Global Workplace: 2023 Report.* Washing-

ton, D.C.: Gallup, Inc., 2023. https://www.gallup.com/workplace/349484/state-of-the-global-workplace.aspx

8. McKinsey & Company. "Great Attrition or Great Attraction? The Choice Is Yours." September 2021. https://www.mckinsey.com/capabilities/people-and-organizational-performance/our-insights/the-great-attrition-is-making-hiring-harder-are-you-searching-the-right-talent-pools

9. Bachelder, Cheryl. *Dare to Serve: How to Drive Superior Results by Serving Others.* Oakland, CA: Berrett-Koehler Publishers, 2015.

Chapter Four

1. Gallup. "State of the Global Workplace 2023 Report." Gallup, 2023.

2. Rosenthal, Robert, and Lenore Jacobson. *Pygmalion in the Classroom: Teacher Expectation and Pupils' Intellectual Development.* Holt, Rinehart and Winston, 1968.

3. Cameron, Kim S., Jane E. Dutton, and Robert E. Quinn, eds. *Positive Organizational Scholarship: Foundations of a New Discipline.* Berrett-Koehler Publishers, 2003.

4. Kouzes, James M., and Barry Z. Posner. *Encouraging the Heart: A Leader's Guide to Rewarding and Recognizing Others.* Jossey-Bass, 2003.

Chapter Five

1. Bandura, Albert. *Social Learning Theory.* Englewood Cliffs, NJ: Prentice Hall, 1977.

2. Dweck, Carol S. *Mindset: The New Psychology of Success.* New York: Random House, 2006.

3. Gallup. "State of the Global Workplace 2023 Report." Gallup, Inc. 2023.

4. Workplace Accountability Study. "The Workplace Accountability Index." Partners in Leadership, 2023.

5. Hersey, Paul, and Ken Blanchard. *Management of Organiza-*

tional Behavior: Utilizing Human Resources. Englewood Cliffs, NJ: Prentice-Hall, 1982.

Chapter Six

1. Anderson, Cameron, Stéphane Côté, and Dacher Keltner. "The Experience of Power: Examining the Effects of Power on Approach and Inhibition Tendencies." *Journal of Personality and Social Psychology* 83, no. 6 (2003): 1362–1377.

2. Collins, Jim. *Good to Great: Why Some Companies Make the Leap… and Others Don't.* New York: HarperBusiness, 2001.

3. Gallup. "State of the Global Workplace: 2023 Report." Gallup, 2023. https://www.gallup.com/workplace.

4. Schein, Edgar H. *Humble Inquiry: The Gentle Art of Asking Instead of Telling.* San Francisco: Berrett-Koehler Publishers, 2013.

Chapter Seven

1. Eva, Nathan, et al. "Servant Leadership: A Systematic Review and Call for Future Research." *The Leadership Quarterly* 30, no. 1 (2019): 111–132.

2. Gallup. *State of the Global Workplace 2023 Report.* Gallup, Inc., 2023.

3. Greenleaf, Robert K. *Servant Leadership: A Journey into the Nature of Legitimate Power and Greatness.* Paulist Press, 1977.

4. van Dierendonck, Dirk. "Servant Leadership: A Review and Synthesis." *Journal of Management* 37, no. 4 (2011): 1228–1261.

Chapter Eight

1. Brownell, Judi. *Listening: Attitudes, Principles, and Skills.* 5th ed. New York: Routledge, 2012.

2. Harvard Business Review. "The Power of Listening." *Harvard Business Review,* July 14, 2016. https://hbr.org/2016/07/the-power-of-listening.

3. "The Importance of Listening in Leadership." *Journal of Applied Psychology* 101, no. 6 (2016): 831–845.

Chapter Nine

1. Brown, Brené. *Dare to Lead: Brave Work. Tough Conversations. Whole Hearts.* New York: Random House, 2018.
2. Carson, Rachel. *Silent Spring.* Boston: Houghton Mifflin, 1962.
3. Dweck, Carol S. *Mindset: The New Psychology of Success.* New York: Ballantine Books, 2006.
4. Harvard Business Review. "The Future of Leadership: Courageous Leaders Win." Harvard Business Review, January-February 2019. https://hbr.org/2019/01/the-future-of-leadership-courageous-leaders-win.

Chapter Ten

1. Brown, Brené. *Dare to Lead: Brave Work. Tough Conversations. Whole Hearts.* New York: Random House, 2018.
2. Cuddy, Amy J. C. "Your Body Language Shapes Who You Are." *Harvard Business Review*, October 2012. https://hbr.org/2012/10/your-body-language-shapes-who-you-are.
3. Goleman, Daniel. *Emotional Intelligence: Why It Can Matter More Than IQ.* New York: Bantam Books, 1995.
4. Goldsmith, Marshall, and Mark Reiter. *What Got You Here Won't Get You There: How Successful People Become Even More Successful.* New York: Hyperion, 2007.
5. Harvard Business Review. "Leadership Under Pressure." *Harvard Business Review Analytical Services Report*, 2019. https://hbr.org/resources/pdfs/comm/dale-carnegie/LeadershipUnderPressure.pdf.
6. Weil, Andrew. *Spontaneous Happiness.* New York: Little, Brown and Company, 2011.

Chapter Eleven

1. Buckingham, Marcus, and Ashley Goodall. *Nine Lies About Work: A Freethinking Leader's Guide to the Real World.* Boston: Harvard Business Review Press, 2019.

2. Csikszentmihalyi, Mihaly. *Flow: The Psychology of Optimal Experience*. New York: Harper Perennial Modern Classics, 2008.

3. Gallup, Inc. *State of the American Workplace Report*. Washington, DC: Gallup, 2017.

4. Lencioni, Patrick. *The Advantage: Why Organizational Health Trumps Everything Else in Business*. San Francisco: Jossey-Bass, 2012.

5. Sinek, Simon. *Start With Why: How Great Leaders Inspire Everyone to Take Action*. New York: Portfolio, 2009.

6. Harvard Business Review. *HBR Guide to Thinking Strategically*. Boston: Harvard Business Review Press, 2018.

Chapter Twelve

1. Bandura, Albert. *Self-Efficacy: The Exercise of Control*. New York: W.H. Freeman, 1997.

2. Stajkovic, Alexander D., and Fred Luthans. "Self-Efficacy and Work-Related Performance: A Meta-Analysis." *Psychological Bulletin* 124, no. 2 (1998): 240–261. https://doi.org/10.1037/0033-2909.124.2.240.

Chapter Thirteen

1. Colquitt, Jason A. "On the Dimensionality of Organizational Justice: A Construct Validation of a Measure." *Journal of Applied Psychology* 86, no. 3 (2001): 386–400.

2. Duhigg, Charles. *Smarter Faster Better: The Secrets of Being Productive in Life and Business*. New York: Random House, 2016. (Cites findings from Google's Project Aristotle).

3. Edmondson, Amy C. "Psychological Safety and Learning Behavior in Work Teams." *Administrative Science Quarterly* 44, no. 2 (1999): 350–383.

4. Mehrabian, Albert. *Silent Messages: Implicit Communication of Emotions and Attitudes*. Belmont, CA: Wadsworth, 1971.

5. Rock, David, and Jeffrey Schwartz. "The Neuroscience of Leadership." *Strategy+Business* 43 (Summer 2006): 1–10. https://www.strategy-business.com/article/06207.

Chapter Fourteen

1. Porath, Christine. "Make Civility the Norm on Your Team."

Harvard Business Review, January 2014. https://hbr.org/2014/01/make-civility-the-norm-on-your-team.

2. Dutton, Jane E. "Leading Respectfully." *Leader to Leader* 2011, no. 62 (Spring 2011): 45–51.

3. Edmondson, Amy C. *The Fearless Organization: Creating Psychological Safety in the Workplace for Learning, Innovation, and Growth*. Hoboken, NJ: Wiley, 2019.

4. Grant, Adam. *Give and Take: Why Helping Others Drives Our Success*. New York: Penguin Books, 2014.

5. Frost, Peter J., and Sandra Robinson. "The Toxic Handler: Organizational Hero—and Casualty." *Harvard Business Review*, July-August 1999.

6. Schein, Edgar H. *Organizational Culture and Leadership*. 5th ed. Hoboken, NJ: John Wiley & Sons, 2017.

Chapter Fifteen

1. Barrett, Lisa Feldman. *How Emotions Are Made: The Secret Life of the Brain*. Boston: Houghton Mifflin Harcourt, 2017.

2. Duhigg, Charles. "What Google Learned From Its Quest to Build the Perfect Team." *The New York Times Magazine*, February 25, 2016. https://www.nytimes.com/2016/02/28/magazine/what-google-learned-from-its-quest-to-build-the-perfect-team.html.

3. Edmondson, Amy C. *The Fearless Organization: Creating Psychological Safety in the Workplace for Learning, Innovation, and Growth*. Hoboken, NJ: Wiley, 2018.

4. Goleman, Daniel. *Emotional Intelligence: Why It Can Matter More Than IQ*. New York: Bantam Books, 2006.

5. Lencioni, Patrick. *The Advantage: Why Organizational Health Trumps Everything Else in Business*. San Francisco: Jossey-Bass, 2012.

6. Sinek, Simon. *Leaders Eat Last: Why Some Teams Pull Together and Others Don't*. New York: Portfolio, 2014.

Chapter Sixteen

1. DDI. *High-Resolution Leadership: A Synthesis of 15,000 Assess-*

ments into How Leaders Shape Business Success. Development Dimensions International, 2016.

2. Edmondson, Amy C. "Psychological Safety and Learning Behavior in Work Teams." *Administrative Science Quarterly* 44, no. 2 (1999): 350–83.

3. Ophir, Eyal, Clifford Nass, and Anthony D. Wagner. "Cognitive Control in Media Multitaskers." *Proceedings of the National Academy of Sciences* 106, no. 37 (2009): 15583–87. https://doi.org/10.1073/pnas.0903620106.

4. Rogers, Carl R. *On Becoming a Person: A Therapist's View of Psychotherapy.* Boston: Houghton Mifflin, 1961.

Chapter Seventeen

1. Lee, A., Willis, S., & Tian, A. W. (2018). *Empowering leadership: A meta-analytic examination of incremental contribution, mediation, and moderation.* Journal of Organizational Behavior, 39(3), 306–325. https://doi.org/10.1002/job.2220

2. Pink, Daniel H. *Drive: The Surprising Truth About What Motivates Us.* New York: Riverhead Books, 2009.

3. Thomas, K. W., & Velthouse, B. A. (1990). *Cognitive elements of empowerment: An "interpretive" model of intrinsic task motivation.* Academy of Management Review, 15(4), 666–681.

4. Amabile, T. M., & Kramer, S. J. (2011). *The Progress Principle: Using Small Wins to Ignite Joy, Engagement, and Creativity at Work.* Boston: Harvard Business Review Press.

5. Grant, A. M. (2013). *Give and Take: Why Helping Others Drives Our Success.* New York: Viking.

6. Yukl, G. (2013). *Leadership in Organizations.* 8th ed. Boston: Pearson Education.

Chapter Eighteen

1. Dweck, Carol S. *Mindset: The New Psychology of Success.* New York: Random House, 2006.

2. Edmondson, Amy C. "Psychological Safety and Learning Behavior in Work Teams." *Administrative Science Quarterly* 44, no. 2 (1999): 350–383. https://doi.org/10.2307/2666999

3. Schein, Edgar H. *Humble Inquiry: The Gentle Art of Asking Instead of Telling.* San Francisco: Berrett-Koehler Publishers, 2013.

4. Grant, Adam. *Think Again: The Power of Knowing What You Don't Know.* New York: Viking, 2021.

5. Brown, Brené. *Dare to Lead: Brave Work. Tough Conversations. Whole Hearts.* New York: Random House, 2018.

6. Tannenbaum, Scott I., and Christopher Cerasoli. "Do Team Debriefs Improve Team Effectiveness? A Meta-Analysis." *Human Factors* 55, no. 1 (2013): 231–245.

7. Reeves, Martin, and Jack Fuller. "We Need Imagination Now More Than Ever." *Harvard Business Review*, April 2020. https://hbr.org/2020/04/we-need-imagination-now-more-than-ever

Chapter Nineteen

1. Duckworth, Angela. *Grit: The Power of Passion and Perseverance.* New York: Scribner, 2016.

2. Maslach, Christina, and Michael P. Leiter. *The Truth About Burnout: How Organizations Cause Personal Stress and What to Do About It.* San Francisco: Jossey-Bass, 1997.

3. Luthans, Fred, Carolyn M Youssef, and Bruce J. Avolio. *Psychological Capital: Developing the Human Competitive Edge.* Oxford: Oxford University Press, 2007.

4. Sutcliffe, Kathleen M., and Timothy J. Vogus. "Organizing for Resilience." In *Positive Organizational Scholarship*, edited by Kim S. Cameron, Jane E. Dutton, and Robert E. Quinn, 94–110. San Francisco: Berrett-Koehler, 2003.

5. Southwick, Steven M., and Dennis S. Charney. *Resilience: The Science of Mastering Life's Greatest Challenges.* Cambridge: Cambridge University Press, 2018.

Chapter Twenty

1. Coughlan, Peter, and Betsy Morris. "The Leader as Coach." *Harvard Business Review*, January–February 2014. https://hbr.org/2014/01/the-leader-as-coach.

2. Spreitzer, Gretchen M., Christine Porath, Cristina Gibson, and Deborah Garnett. "Thriving at Work: Toward Its Measure-

ment, Construct Validation, and Theoretical Refinement." *Journal of Organizational Behavior* 26, no. 5 (2005): 529–45. https://doi.org/10.1002/job.343.

3. Drucker, Peter F. *The Essential Drucker*. New York: Harper Business, 2001.

4. Catmull, Ed. *Creativity, Inc.: Overcoming the Unseen Forces That Stand in the Way of True Inspiration*. New York: Random House, 2014.

5. Angelou, Maya. *Wouldn't Take Nothing for My Journey Now*. New York: Bantam, 1993.

AUTHOR BIOGRAPHY

Ron Harvey is an internationally respected leadership expert, executive coach, keynote speaker, and the Vice President & COO of Global Core Strategies & Consulting, a firm dedicated to helping leaders and organizations unlock their full powerful potential.

A U.S. Army veteran, Ron brings over three decades of real-world leadership experience—from the front lines of military service to the boardrooms of Fortune 500 companies, nonprofit organizations, and government agencies.

Known for his ability to connect with audiences across industries, Ron has coached CEOs, executives, educators, and community leaders, guiding them to lead with purpose, influence with integrity, and create lasting impact. His work has taken him into high-stakes environments, where he has helped leaders navigate cultural transformation, strengthen team trust, and sustain performance during times of rapid change.

Ron's philosophy is simple but powerful: *Leadership is not about the position you hold—it's about the impact you have on the lives of others. People Always Matter!*

This belief has shaped his approach to leadership development, blending practical strategies with compelling storytelling to help leaders inspire trust, cultivate resilience, and build legacies worth remembering.

As a speaker, Ron has shared the stage with influential leaders from business, education, and government, delivering engaging, actionable, and transformative presentations that leave audiences equipped to lead at a higher level. His clients span industries from aviation and healthcare to manufacturing and education, and his work has directly influenced leaders in the U.S. and abroad.

Beyond the boardroom, Ron serves on the boards of the South Carolina Center for Fathers and Families, the Greater Columbia Chamber of Commerce, and Serve and Connect. He is deeply committed to empowering communities, advocating for sustainable leadership, and mentoring the next generation of leaders.

Ron is also the host of the *UnPacked with Ron Harvey* leadership podcast, where he interviews thought leaders and innovators on what it takes to lead with authenticity and create meaningful change. He is the author of *Turning Point Leadership: Moving From Success to Significance,* a book that challenges leaders to focus on the human qualities that foster influence, connection, and long-term success.

When he's not speaking, coaching, or writing, Ron can be found investing in his family, mentoring young leaders, and reminding everyone he meets that *People Always Matter.*

Made in the USA
Columbia, SC
16 September 2025